DAVID O. McKAY LIBRARY

D0933795

APR 10 2002

WITHDRAWN

JUN 2 4 2024

DAVID O. McKAY LIBRARY
BYU-IDAHO

PROPERTY OF:
DAVID O. McKAY LIBRARY
BYU-IDAHO
REXBURG ID 83460-0405

The WISDOM *of* SOLOMON *at* WORK

Other Books by the Authors

The New SuperLeadership: Leading Others to Lead Themselves
Charles C. Manz and Henry P. Sims, Jr.
(Berrett-Koehler, 2001)

Team Work and Group Dynamics
Gregory Stewart, Charles C. Manz, and Henry P. Sims, Jr.
(Wiley, 1999)

The Leadership Wisdom of Jesus
Charles C. Manz
(Berrett-Koehler, 1998; soft-cover, 1999)

For Team Members Only:
Making Your Workplace Team Productive and Hassle-Free
Charles C. Manz, Christopher P. Neck,
James Mancuso, and Karen P. Manz
(AMACOM, 1997)

Medicine for the Mind: Healing Words to Help You Soar
Christopher P. Neck
(McGraw-Hill, 1997)

Company of Heroes: Unleashing the Power of Self-Leadership
Henry P. Sims, Jr. and Charles C. Manz
(Wiley, 1996)

Business Without Bosses:
How Self-Managing Teams Are Building High Performance Companies
Charles C. Manz and Henry P. Sims, Jr.
(Wiley, 1993; soft-cover, 1995)

Mastering Self-Leadership: Empowering Yourselves for Personal Excellence
Charles C. Manz
(Prentice-Hall, 1992;
Second Edition with Christopher P. Neck, 1999)

Management Live! The Video Book
Robert D. Marx, Todd Jick, and Peter Frost
(Prentice-Hall, 1991)

Superleadership: Leading Others to Lead Themselves
Charles C. Manz and Henry P. Sims, Jr.
(Prentice-Hall, 1989; soft-cover, Berkley Books, 1990)

The Art of Self-Leadership:
Strategies for Personal Effectiveness in Your Life and Work
Charles C. Manz
(Prentice-Hall, 1983)

The WISDOM *of* SOLOMON *at* WORK

ANCIENT VIRTUES FOR LIVING AND LEADING TODAY

Charles C. Manz

Karen P. Manz

Robert D. Marx

Christopher P. Neck

BERRETT-KOEHLER PUBLISHERS, INC.
San Francisco

© 2001 by Charles C. Manz, Karen P. Manz, Robert D. Marx, and Christopher P. Neck.
All rights reserved. No part of this publication may be reproduced, distributed, or transmitted in any form or by any means, including photocopying, recording, or other electronic or mechanical methods, without the prior written permission of the publisher, except in the case of brief quotations embodied in critical reviews and certain other noncommercial uses permitted by copyright law. For permission requests, write to the publisher, addressed "Attention: Permissions Coordinator," at the address below.

Berrett-Koehler Publishers, Inc.
450 Sansome Street, Suite 1200
San Francisco, CA 94111-3320
Tel: 415-288-0260   Fax: 415-362-2512
Website: www.bkconnection.com

ORDERING INFORMATION

Individual sales. Berrett-Koehler publications are available through most bookstores. They can also be ordered direct from Berrett-Koehler Publishers by calling, toll-free: 800-929-2929; fax 802-864-7626.

Quantity sales. Special discounts are available on quantity purchases by corporations, associations, and others. For details, contact the "Special Sales Department" at the Berrett-Koehler address above.

Orders for college textbook/course adoption use. Please contact Berrett-Koehler Publishers toll-free: 800-929-2929; fax 802-864-7626.

Orders by U.S. trade bookstores and wholesalers. Please contact Publishers Group West, 1700 Fourth Street, Berkeley, CA 94710; 510-528-1444; 1-800-788-3123; fax 510-528-9555.

Printed in the United States of America

Printed on acid-free and recycled paper that is composed of 85 percent recovered fiber, including 10 percent postconsumer waste.

Library of Congress Cataloging-in-Publication Data

The wisdom of Solomon at work : ancient virtues for living
and leading today / Charles C. Manz . . . [et al.].
        p.   cm.
Includes bibliographical references and index.
ISBN 1-57675-085-X
1. Leadership—Biblical teaching.   2. Success—Biblical teaching.   3. Work—Biblical
teaching.   4. Bible. O.T.—Criticism, interpretation, etc.   I. Manz, Charles C.
BS1199.L4 W57   2001
284.4—dc21   2001025390

06   05   04   03   02   01   10   9   8   7   6   5   4   3   2   1

Designed by Detta Penna

*We dedicate this book
to our grandparents*

CONTENTS

∞

∞

God gave Solomon very great wisdom, discernment, and breadth of understanding as vast as the sand on the seashore, so that Solomon's wisdom surpassed the wisdom of all the people of the east, and all the wisdom of Egypt. He was wiser than anyone else. . . his fame spread throughout all the surrounding nations. He composed three thousand proverbs, and his songs numbered a thousand and five. He would speak of trees, from the cedar that is in the Lebanon to the hyssop that grows in the wall; he would speak of animals, and birds, and reptiles, and fish. People came from all the nations to hear the wisdom of Solomon; they came from all the kings of the earth who had heard of his wisdom. (I Kings 4:29-34)*

---

*The scripture quotations contained herein are from *The New Revised Standard Version Bible* copyright ©1989 by the Division of Christian Education of the National Council of the Churches of Christ in the U.S.A. Used by permission. All rights reserved.

PREFACE

∞

The search for wisdom is a daunting challenge that can draw us to several possible paths. In the days of Solomon, the search for wisdom led to the palace of a legendary wise and prosperous king. Where do we search for wisdom today? Ask our kids where we should look and they might say to call up "Wisdom.com." Ask our parents, and they might say that we should enroll in the "school of hard knocks" via the Great Depression or another major life challenge. Ask our boss, and she might say to look at the quarterly report or the corporate mission statement. In truth, each of these suggestions hold some merit, but there is much more to this search.

At the dawn of our new century and millennium, as in the days of Solomon, it is appropriate to stop and reflect on where we are and where we are going. As we continue to enter the great unknown, many of us feel a special need for wisdom. The world is undergoing such rapid change that it would be easy just to be swept along by the tide.

We believe the search for wisdom is a journey that can be significantly assisted by useful questions and personal reflection. There is no quick-fix shortcut to wisdom and no substitute for deep reflection. There are no easy answers, but we believe that each of us can move toward wisdom in our life. Perhaps the best way to view this book is as a context for asking questions and reflecting as you traverse the uncertain terrain of wisdom in work and life.

The Wisdom of Solomon at Work points to places along the journey that are very much a part of the human condition in life and work. It looks at the challenges of finding the belief and trust necessary to undertake the journey and the courage to stay the course. It also explores virtues that enable us to look beyond ourselves as we serve and lead.

The seeds of this book arose as we thought about our own life stories and the key issues we authors have faced in work and life. We felt a shared concern with many of our contemporaries for achieving better understanding in a changing world and for making healthier connections with others. We also recognized a desire among us to make meaningful contributions, especially through our work. We understood all of this to be part of the search for wisdom in life.

We then looked to sources of wisdom, both ancient and contemporary, that are drawn primarily from stories of the human condition. We began with the most common Judeo-Christian symbol of wisdom in antiquity, the wisdom of Solomon. As we read the stories of Solomon in the Hebrew Bible (commonly called the Old Testament), we were impressed by the possibilities that this ancient wisdom might offer for today's worklife.

Reading the tales of Solomon led us to think about other Old Testament characters whose stories epitomize basic virtues for a meaningful life. These included the faith of Job, the courage of David, the compassion of Ruth, and the integrity and justice of Moses. Each of these biblical characters struggled faithfully to find meaning in their lives, and some made mistakes that are easily translatable to contemporary behaviors.

As we delved into the struggles and triumphs of each of these biblical characters, we realized that each of them contributed to an aspect of wisdom. *This resulted in our development of a wisdom framework that we identify as the wisdom of*

Solomon. To focus on Solomon's celebrated wisdom without building a foundation from the stories of his forebears would be like going to the end of a story without tracing the events that led up to it.

The stories of these biblical characters raised a variety of issues, and these issues became the titles of our essays. The issues these biblical characters faced are issues we face today in our own worklife. The contexts are different, interpretations may vary, but at a deeper level—perhaps at the level of wisdom—we can begin to see an enduring quality of the human condition. Each chapter provides points for reflection on an aspect of the wisdom of Solomon and poses a poignant question raised by each character's story.

Each character was of particular interest to some member of the author team. You will notice a variety of writing styles as we respond to the core issues and questions raised by each character in relation to the search for wisdom. We tried to capture the essence of issues and questions that emerge from each biblical character's story in relation to a virtue of the wisdom of Solomon and to contemporary worklife. We hope this inspires you to ask questions about your own life and work.

It is not our intention to portray ourselves as biblical scholars who have a special understanding of the details and controversies surrounding these stories. We are laypersons, not theologians. We are immersed in our own life journeys. We connect to the search for wisdom from our experiences, of which our faith journeys are a significant part. If you are inspired to study further, there are well-written commentaries available, and of course the original Hebrew Bible is there for your exploration.

Finally, each of our selected characters, Job, David, Ruth, Moses, and Solomon, had a profound faith in their God. It is not our intention to convince you or dissuade you about belief in any particular religious or spiritual being. The Hebrew biblical characters who form the foundation of our wisdom framework, however, do indicate that a deeper faith in life beyond ourselves is at the heart of wisdom. So, step back from the stockmarket, from your PC and its *wisdom.com*, and join our search for the wisdom of Solomon.

Acknowledgments

We have been fortunate to have had many sources of wisdom and support in the preparation of this book. We recognize the many individuals who have contributed to our developing understanding. These include Rabbi Harold Kushner, Dr. Judith Neal, Dr. Susan Niditch, the Reverend Robert Mitchell, Dr. Robert Alvarez, the Reverend Charles Barner, Dr. Donna Queeney, Dr. Peter Hom, Dr. Vikas Anand, Dr. Greg Stewart, Dr. Frank Shipper, Dr. Hank Sims, and Rabbi Saul Perlmutter of UMass Hillel. Each of these people has affected our thinking and writing about spirituality at work.

We are also very grateful to those who inspired our writing because of their rich perspectives and the ways they have chosen to live wisely. Most notably we acknowledge Charles Nirenberg, Aaron Feuerstein, Steven Piersanti, and Dr. David K. Scott. We also thank the helpful people at Berrett-Koehler Publishers who challenged us to make this a better book.

In addition, we thank our universities, the University of Massachusetts Amherst and Virginia Polytechnic Institute and State University. Our thanks extend to our deans and chairs, Dean Tom O'Brien and Dr. Linda Smircich at the Isenberg School of Management, and Dr. Richard Sorensen and Dr. Jon Shepard at the Pamplin College of Business. The Administrative Resources Center, and especially Becky Jerome, at UMass Amherst were very helpful in facilitating the preparation of this manuscript.

Charles Manz would like to offer a special thanks to Charles and Janet Nirenberg, whose generous gift made possible his current position as the Nirenberg Professor of Business Leadership. Karen Manz would like to thank the planning committee of the national conference, "Going Public with Spirituality in Work and Higher Education," held at the University of Massachusetts Amherst June 4-6, 2000. Bob Marx would like to acknowledge Rabbi Sheila Weinberg and her congregation, the Jewish Community of Amherst. And we all thank the companies, managers, and employees upon whose inspiration we draw to highlight examples of *The Wisdom of Solomon at Work*.

Finally, we thank our families, who provide the fertile ground for learning how to live with wisdom and challenge.

Introduction

The seeker of wisdom physically collapsed, groaned with relief, and gazed upon the white-haired old man sitting on the peak of the great mountain. Pausing for a moment to look cautiously over the shear cliff that had been climbed, the seeker gasped, "Old man, I have struggled on the side of this mountain for days to be able to speak with you, because many have said that you are among the wisest of all the living. I must know, What is the true nature of life?"

The white-haired old man responded with a question of his own. "Tell me first, how do you see life, my child?"

The seeker looked away frowning and said slowly and sadly, "I believe that life beats us down, that people use and discard one another, and that challenge and hardship suck the very spirit out of us all. There is little hope that anything will ever change." Turning to the old man, the seeker asked with an anguished voice,

"Is this the nature of life?"

"Yes," responded the old man. "This is the nature of life, my child."

The seeker's head dropped with a weighted gaze toward the ground. Slowly rising, the seeker turned and solemnly began a descent of the cliff.

Later in the day, another seeker struggled over the edge of the cliff and collapsed at the feet of the white-haired old man. "Tell me, old man of much wisdom," the seeker gasped, "What is the nature of life?" The old man again asked the question, "Tell me first, how do you see life, my child?"

At this question, the seeker looked hopefully into the old man's eyes. "Life can be hard and the way is often difficult, but I believe the nature of life is basically good. People are not perfect, but I see much value in the heart of each person I meet, even those who would be called the most lowly. I believe that life is challenge and growth and offers a sweet victory for those who try and endure." The seeker paused with a hopeful stare into the old man's eyes. "Is this the nature of life?"

"Yes," responded the old man, "This is the nature of life, my child."[1]

A CALL FOR WISDOM
IN WORK AND LIFE

∞

What is the nature of life for you? Are you economically prosperous, yet in some way haunted by a lack of meaningful purpose in your work and life? Do you feel a need to infuse more of a sense of spirit into your daily routine? Do you long for "something more"?

This book can best be described as a collection of personal essays designed to help shed light on these kinds of questions; it draws inspiration from what is arguably one of the most powerful sources of wisdom in the world, the ancient Hebrew scriptures. We draw from this font as our source of inspiration for reflections on our personal journeys and we sincerely hope it will help you with yours. Ultimately, infusing a spiritual component into our daily lives is a highly personal challenge that cannot be driven by any quick-fix, simple prescriptions. There are no substitutes for personal struggle and reflection. Nevertheless, we strongly believe it is a worthwhile pursuit and a badly needed one, especially given the increasingly turbulent, unsettling, and all-too-often isolating world in which we live.

Stop and think for a moment. Do you feel as if you live in a rapidly changing landscape where what worked yesterday is obsolete tomorrow? Where the only thing that stays the same is change, and that most of what you learned growing up no longer fits this life? And, whether you think you are getting ahead financially in your career or not, do you feel increasingly isolated and unsatisfied with your relationships and sense of meaning in life? What's going on?

Life is going on. It is reshaping before our eyes, rapidly at times, in ways never before experienced in human history. The form and purpose of many aspects of our lives are being called into question. Much of this transition is tied to the effects of changing technology and movement toward a global perspective. How and what we learn is being driven by fundamental changes, like the Internet. Knowledge is becoming the largest economic commodity. And, while we may enjoy increasing efficiencies and productivity from faster and more powerful technologies, we often find our sense of connection and relationships in cold computer screens and multi-color websites.

The business world is also transitioning in response to both technological revolution and globalization. The workplace is seeing a steady increase in self-employed or free-agent individuals, telecommuters, and new job categories arising to meet the emerging techni-global market. Job security as we have known it has become, for many, just a memory.

At a time when our business organizations are becoming more and more attuned to the financial realities of a global and highly competitive economy, our social fabric is experiencing an equally profound upheaval. Families, schools, government, and churches are in flux. It seems as though we are balancing precariously on a rolling log floating down a foggy river. We can't see where we are going and we feel a desperate need to get our feet on solid ground!

Yet in the midst of this, we are in a time of economic prosperity and of the resurgence of spirituality. Although membership in mainline religious denominations continues to decline, the yearning for some sort of stability and meaning is being played out in the workplace. During the past decade, a proliferation of books, conferences, and speakers has focused on spirituality in the workplace. The idea of "doing well by doing good"—making money while contributing to the betterment of society—has been incorporated into many companies' mission and practice.

We are in a time of heightened spiritual awareness. And, as we travel through the new millennium in an increasingly complex and changing world, we believe there is no place in greater need of spirit and wisdom than the workplace.

In this book we explore ancient spiritual writings contained in the Hebrew Bible with a special focus on the concept of wisdom. In Hebrew scriptures, wisdom was God's first creation, and it is frequently associated with a sense of awe for the greatness and power of God. This awe, we believe, is spiritual and it drives the search within us for something better, something that connects us all and helps us to discover our true selves.

The source of ancient wisdom chosen for this book is scripture from the Old Testament, or Hebrew Bible. We found that it contains a rich set of stories that offers inspiration and insights for a spiritual, yet practical, quest. Part of our reason for choosing this source is that our team of authors represents religious heritage in the Jewish, Catholic, and Protestant traditions, all of which have Hebrew roots. This is an ancient source of wisdom in which we shared a common ground.

At the same time, we recognized that a strength of our author team was the diversity of our backgrounds and experiences. This led us to decide at the outset to allow our original writings to flow naturally from our own personal thoughts and conclusions. Thus, you will find a rich mix of styles and ideas throughout the book. We hope you will find this variety to be both interesting and enlightening. The biblical writings served as the catalyst for our own reflective search for an expanded view of life and work with spirit.

We selected the stories of five characters in the Old Testament, written over three millennia ago, as enduring sources that describe the human condition. These characters were chosen as our source of inspiration, not because they comprise an exhaustive list of what is necessary to be open to wisdom, but because each character personifies a spiritual virtue that we believe plays a significant role in the search for wisdom. The five characters and their respective virtues are the faith of Job, the courage of David, the compassion of Ruth, the integrity and justice of Moses, and the wisdom of Solomon.

You may never have seriously encountered these stories, or you may be returning to what you have known in your childhood. We do not intend this book to be specifically religious, nor do we expect you necessarily to be familiar with or practicing in the Judeo-Christian tradition. We use the biblical scriptures as a source of inspiration for thinking about wise living and working in today's world.

We have brought our own spirituality, life experiences, and professional expertise into the reading of the scriptures. The reading is highly interpretive; it is not that there is any one meaning we aim to extract. Rather, there are many meanings. We do not attempt to review these stories from a critical theological viewpoint. Rather, we draw upon them as a starting point for personal reflections that we hope will be useful to you in your own journey. The scriptural citations are included for you to pursue on your own if you desire to gain greater insight into a character's story.

In our search of sources, we then shifted our focus from

ancient to contemporary wisdom. We specifically looked to the workplace for organizations and leaders who acted with foresight and wisdom to put the welfare of their employees and customers first. Companies that focus beyond short-term profits are realizing many human, as well as financial, benefits. We looked for examples of leaders and companies that have discovered that taking a broader, wiser view of immediate challenges can lead to acting with integrity while achieving bottom-line gains.

Throughout the book we will share the examples of a number of leaders and companies. In particular, we highlight the ethical story of Aaron Feuerstein, CEO of Malden Mills, as an example of far-sighted leadership wisdom in practice. Feuerstein's story illustrates connections we are attempting to make in this book between ancient and contemporary wisdom and our work world.

The Malden Mills case is centered on the personal wisdom and remarkable leadership Feuerstein displayed in response to the devastating 1995 fire that destroyed much of his textile company. Aaron Feuerstein is a devout Jew who places great importance on the wisdom and guidance for his work and life that is contained in the Hebrew scriptures: "The Old Testament is in my innards," he told us.[2]

In leading Malden Mills through its rebuilding process, and thus ensuring the economic security of Lawrence, Massachusetts, Feuerstein provides a contemporary story of a leader who reconciles faith, courage, compassion, integrity, justice, and wisdom (the virtues addressed in this book) with business values. At the same time, Feuerstein embodies very human characteristics, including the kinds of weaknesses with which we all personally struggle. His story is not a fairy tale, and his company and employees have struggled with significant problems and conflicts before and since the fire. Nevertheless, in the wake of that devastating fire, Aaron Feuerstein provided a vivid real-life example of spiritually grounded, yet highly effective, business leadership.

Thus, we begin our search for wisdom by examining the extraordinary story of Aaron Feuerstein, CEO of Malden Mills, a company that produces fabric in a historic New England mill town. Feuerstein is a successful businessman who has kept his eye on his people while, with one foot, he tries to balance on the rolling log of global competition in the textile industry and, with the other foot, he is firmly planted on the land of the Old Testament.

THE CASE OF MALDEN MILLS

∞

In the darkest of night skies, a fire raged out of control at Malden Mills, a synthetic textile and upholstery plant in Lawrence/Methuen, Massachusetts, blue-collar towns with a combined population of 110,000. Before it was over it would be described as the worst industrial fire ever in Massachusetts, injuring at least thirty-three workers, thirteen severely, and rendering most of the buildings useless while leaving over 1000 of the 2800 employees without a workplace.[3]

That night, Aaron Feuerstein, the owner of Malden Mills, was celebrating the milestone of his seventieth birthday with his family at a nearby restaurant, unaware of the fire that was consuming his business. The festivities ended abruptly when Feuerstein returned home to the ominous late-night ring of the telephone. "The mill's burning, Aaron. The whole mill's on fire!" were the words of his anguished manager at the scene of the fire.

A shaken but determined Aaron Feuerstein stood before the conflagration that was destroying what had taken his family generations to build. For a moment it seemed as if all of life's forces were surrounding him at once: the heat of the fire, the cold of the winter, the celebration of his birthday, and the destruction of his life's work. His focus settled on the condition of his critically burned employees and the courage that he must summon to face his people and himself.

As the flames consumed building after building in the early hours of December 12, Aaron Feuerstein noticed that the roof of Malden Mills' remaining manufacturing building, Finishing 2, was being licked by flames. Looking for any positives in this dreadful disaster, Feuerstein told his head engineer "You know, we might get lucky. That building might not burn."

"Don't kid yourselves, Aaron," was the expert's reply. "You haven't got a chance in hell. By tomorrow morning it'll be gone just like everything else."[4]

If Malden Mills were to follow the examples set by most of the textile mills in New England, its owners would collect their insurance money and quietly leave town to relocate in the South or offshore, where there was access to cheaper labor and land. Malden's hapless employees would be left to file for unemployment, search for minimum-wage jobs, or leave the area to find work. With the loss of 3000 jobs, the towns of Lawrence and Methuen would face a grim future. But Feuerstein had already made his decision. "There will be a Malden Mills tomorrow," he vowed, and he went home to an exhausted sleep.

Against all odds, the Finishing 2 building was left standing. Without power, and much of one wall destroyed, it wasn't a pretty sight, but there was one other piece of good news. Several new Polartec (Malden's most profitable product) machines had survived in trailers parked in the smoldering complex and would quickly be up and running in the hastily reconfigured shell of Finishing 2. The survival of Finishing 2 was like Noah's ark in the great flood—a symbol God had given for Feuerstein to begin rebuilding.

A Man of Faith

Stripped of its modern-day details—union contracts, insurance money, bank loans, and global economic pressures—the story of Aaron Feuerstein and Malden Mills is a simple one. A tragedy tests a man's values. Will he decide how to act on the basis of prevailing business practices, or according to the tenets of the commandments of his religious and spiritual traditions?

On the night of the fire and the celebration of his seventieth birthday, Aaron Feuerstein faced such a test. For Feuerstein, a lifetime of faith grounded in the traditions of Judaism had prepared him for moments like this. An important clue to Feuerstein's character can be found in the fact that he had chosen long before the fire to pay his employees well above the industry average. Feuerstein had been taught by his grandfather, a rabbi: "You cannot oppress the wage earner. Each day you must give him his wages." While not following literally the teaching of his elders, Feuerstein clearly invested in his workforce for the long term. Little did he realize how magnificently that investment would pay off for everyone.

For Feuerstein, the connection between his business behavior and his faith is profound. "The essence of the prayers I do in the morning is, 'Hear O Israel, the Lord our God, the Lord is One.'" In reciting this most basic Jewish prayer, the *Shema*, he refers to this oneness as an essential truth. "What I do in business and what I do in the house and what I do in the synagogue should be One." A favorite saying, learned from his father, advised that when everything is in moral chaos you must try your hardest to be a *mensch*, or a man of the highest principles.[5]

Rebuilding from the Remnant

Flying in the face of conventional wisdom, Feuerstein made two memorable decisions that were to inspire his workforce to rebound from their tragic fire. Despite the destruction that lay before him, he immediately decided to keep all his employees on the payroll, even the 1000 who could not work because their worksites were smoldering ruins. With his plant looking reminiscent of a factory destroyed in a World War II bombing run, Feuerstein risked a $1.5 million per week pay-out in salaries and benefits for what came to extend over a 3-month period. By guaranteeing the mostly immigrant work-force their pay and benefits, totaling $15 million, Feuerstein bet his business and his family's fortune on the integrity and loyalty of his employees. Feuerstein did not back away from this difficult situation; rather, he moved toward it with a dedication to his employees, treating them with the dignity he felt they deserved.

But he was not through. When Aaron Feuerstein said, "There will be a Malden Mills tomorrow," he meant that he was going to rebuild Malden Mills in the towns of Lawrence and Methuen. His decision was based on the trusting relationship he had fostered with individual employees and with the community as a whole. "It would have been unconscionable to put 3000 people on the streets and deliver a death blow to the cities of Lawrence and Methuen. . . . It is critically important that our working people have a feeling of belonging," he said, "and not to fear all day long that the company is going to pull the rug out from under them and they'll be out in the street."[6]

More Than Just Profit

But Feuerstein's responsibility to his employees and their community is more than simply good deeds from an elderly executive who was thinking more about his legacy than the bottom line. According to Feuerstein, his is a hard-nosed business strategy that has been successful in the marketplace.

"Malden's profitability strategy is to make its products with a better quality than what's in the marketplace, and it behooves us, if we're looking in the long term, not the short term, for maximum profitability, and to differentiate as best we can from the other people in the marketplace and to distance ourselves by making the very best quality."

He continues: "Now, there's a lot that goes into quality. We attempt to buy the best equipment that we can and put it into the latest state-of-the-art factories. We work really hard with our professional group, with our research and development, with our engineers, with our finance and managerial people. And all of that is critical, otherwise we won't have the quality we need to win the ball game.

"But I know clearly that, when you're all done with all the machinery and all the professional people, in the last analysis it depends on the worker on the floor, the blue-collar guy. And, if he wants you to win, you win the quality battle, and if he wants you to lose, you lose it."

Feuerstein elaborated on how his trusting relationship with his employees was paying dividends: "In spite of the fact that the decision (to rebuild) was made because it was right and not because of the consequences, I'd like to discuss some of the critically favorable consequences that resulted from my decision. The moment that decision was made, in a certain sense my work was over. There was not much more for me to do. My people took over! *They* did it."[7]

We'll Pay You Back Tenfold

Feuerstein beams with pride as he describes the response of his workers. "That Finishing building that was thoroughly burned, in ten days was operating again as a result of the incredible devotion of my own people, who worked twenty-five hours a day and eight days a week.

"And on the happy day they began to produce again, they called me up in my office and said, 'Aaron, please come over and take a look.' So I went down to the plant, walked the corridor, said hello to everyone. And one of the workers came over to me and said, 'Aaron, on behalf of all the workers, I want to thank you, and I also want to tell you that we'll pay you back tenfold.'

"I didn't understand what tenfold meant and how he could do it. I began to understand one month later, when the plant that prior to the fire had produced 130,000 yards a week was now—six weeks after the fire—producing over 200,000 yards per week. And it's only because of the devotion and the loyalty of the workers.

"They were treated correctly, I believe. We like them to treat us right and we have to treat them right. It's a trust. There's a loyalty, and that loyalty can never, never be broken."[8]

The words of mill worker Ramon Garcia seem to capture the employee loyalty that Feuerstein has earned. "I've never seen a guy do as much as he has for people," said Garcia, a native of the Dominican Republic and a nine-year mill veteran. "If you save a job, you save a future. That's what this guy has done for everybody here."[9]

A Model of Wisdom

In the months following the fire, Aaron Feuerstein was honored by the president of the United States and by the governor of his home state of Massachusetts. He received several honorary degrees from universities in recognition for his humanitarian acts.

What continues to amaze him is that, four years after the fire, the invitations to hear his message have not slowed down. Why all this national attention, he wonders, for simply doing the right thing? He seems to have touched a hunger for spiritual leadership in a business environment that primarily values competition and profits.

And to each new audience he addresses, Feuerstein retells the story of Malden Mills. He always emphasizes the loyalty of his workers and his responsibility for treating them right. He speaks to young people about the idea of "oneness," and agonizes over the lessons that his generation of leaders are passing along. "When the younger generation see business-people acting one way in houses of worship and another way in business, they lose faith and confidence in all the preaching that the priests and the ministers and the rabbis are making. They think it's phony. And I think we have to return to the idea of oneness. Not just oneness in words." He ends this thought with an optimistic smile: "But oneness—really, really oneness—and as we do it, the youth of America will have confidence in our integrity."[10]

Postscript

On September 14, 1997, Malden Mills reopened. The new $130-million, state-of-the-art factory stood where the old mill had burned to the ground twenty-one months earlier. Founded in 1906 by Aaron Feuerstein's Hungarian immigrant grandfather, Malden Mills had survived and flourished by adhering to a simple idea that loyalty and profits could go hand-in-hand: business values could be linked to spiritual virtues. With sales up 40% and productivity up 25% since the fire, the future looks bright. For the 15,000 employees, families, and guests attending the dedication, it was hard to hold back the tears as Feuerstein prayed: "I thank you, majestic God of the Universe, for restoring to Malden Mills and its employees our life and soul."[11] He had kept his promise.

IN SEARCH OF THE
WISDOM OF SOLOMON

∞

It is our biological, psychological, and spiritual destiny to search. From the moment of birth, it is our legacy to seek food and safety, to look for novelty rather than boredom, to seek acceptance over rejection. We develop searching strategies that help us to make informed decisions for our lives. We seek and select education or training, a mate, a job, and a place to live. And, as we proceed through the significant stages of our lives, we enter more earnestly into a search for meaning—a deeper sense of understanding ourselves, others, and our world. We seek to know life in a different way. We seek wisdom.

For some, like Aaron Feuerstein, the search for meaning begins early. A set of values emanating from a family philosophy, religious or spiritual belief, or a highly personal set of guidelines for living one's life, is developed. For others, there is less emphasis on developing a philosophy of living. The focus is on the task at hand, what needs to be done and how to do it, rather than on exploring why we are doing what we do. Getting by, or even just surviving, takes precedence over a sense of purpose and meaning. It often takes a life crisis—a serious illness, the death of a loved one, a divorce, a financial setback—to begin the search for meaning and to see ourselves and others in a different light.

During these times of vulnerability, questions of task accomplishment often give way to deeper questions of personal significance and connection. "Have I treated my family, coworkers, and friends in ways of which I can be proud?" "Who am I beyond the work I accomplish?" "Have I made beneficial contributions to the world?" We seek to know in a new and different way how to be better connected with life.

What Is Wisdom?

We ask participants in a workshop to describe characteristics of a person they consider to be wise. Among the many attributes mentioned are humility, integrity, courage, reflectiveness, ability to see the big picture, acquaintance with suffering, empathy, and having a sense of being on a journey. From this we can see that wisdom is both obvious and elusive. For our purposes, we will consider two relatively distinct forms of wisdom: practical and transcendent.

We usually think of wisdom in terms of using superior judgment and following the soundest course of action. It is reflected in action undertaken with insight. Over time, learning from experience results in informed action that is translated into *practical wisdom,* our first type of wisdom. Practical wisdom is comprised of sayings, proverbs, and tidbits of conventional wisdom or common sense. These wisdom guides, and the underlying values upon which they are based, are tied to the need for accomplishing practical life tasks such as working, raising a family, or successfully participating in groups and organizations with business, religious, or other goals.

Practical wisdom emerges as a response to the demands of task accomplishment and relating to others. The form of practical wisdom is often tied to a particular place and time: "Early to bed, early to rise, makes a man healthy, wealthy and wise," "You won't get a good job without a college education," or "Do unto others what you would have them do unto you." Practical wisdom arises within certain *contexts,* such as religion, education, or business. And, invariably, we will witness clashes of practical wisdom systems within these environments. That is, while business wisdom may point to the bottom line as the underlying value of what to do and why, religious wisdom may point to being just at all cost.

The second type of wisdom is *transcendent wisdom.* Transcendent wisdom is a deep form of knowing that flows from reflection upon experience and is sensitive to the details of human encounters with life. In the Judeo-Christian tradition, this wisdom is closely tied to being faithful to God. That is, the focus is beyond oneself and centered within a broader sense of being. Transcendent wisdom is often connected with an intuitive sense of the connection and oneness of all things. It encompasses a broader, longer-term perspective. We encounter transcendent wisdom when we struggle with a way to speak about how we see the world differently. Though elusive and difficult to describe, transcendent wisdom, this deep form of knowing, is the ultimate destination of our search.

In the case of Aaron Feuerstein, the action he took was, in one sense, simple and practical. "We value the worker and community. We rebuild. I behave the same way at work as I do at home. I try consistently to act out of the tenets of my faith." What made his decision to rebuild easier was a lifetime of abiding by a code of conduct spelled out by a spiritual/religious faith. Feuerstein's decision flew in the face of conventional business wisdom. The "wise" thing to do would be to avoid the huge financial risk of rebuilding and instead collect the insurance money and cut his costs.

Ultimately, Feuerstein's action reflects an ability to

traverse the shifting sands of change while remaining anchored to the stable rock of the timeless teachings of his faith. He provides an example that encompasses both practical wisdom (as he draws upon the teachings of his religious tradition) and transcendent (deep knowing) wisdom. The deep knowing emerged from his big-picture, lifelong perspective. Living wisely, to Feuerstein, is not simply a matter of proclaiming "Show me the money!" but includes less obvious riches, such as the fulfillment of rendering service and feeding the human spirit, and other less quantitative nuances of a life journey. "We like them to treat us right and we have to treat them right. It's a trust, and that loyalty can never, never be broken," he says, referring to the relationship he has with his employees.

Wisdom is often assigned a lofty image—something beyond the reach of the ordinary person that requires profound intuition or intellectual ability; this clearly need not be the case. But it does require thoughtful reflection upon our lives, and taking the time to consider the beliefs and values that undergird behavior on a daily basis. A search for greater understanding of the grounding of life and what we are about can be helpful for bringing wisdom within our reach. The seeds of wisdom are planted in the searching.

The Wisdom of Solomon

The wisdom of Solomon is the framework for our wisdom journey. It assimilates the virtues of faith, courage, compassion, integrity, justice, *and* wisdom (more on these virtues later). The wisdom of Solomon is about attempting to live out of these virtues in all contexts of life.

THE WISDOM OF SOLOMON

Wisdom
Justice
Integrity
Compassion
Courage
Faith

The wisdom of Solomon is a holistic perspective that moves us toward a sense of personal integrity where we desire to boldly act out of a set of beliefs and values regardless of the situation in which we find ourselves. Our workplace behavior and values become more congruent with those we assert at home or in our community. We act out of this wisdom perspective for the greater good of ourselves and our surrounding world. And through this process *the wisdom of Solomon* bears fruit as symbolized by the story of King Solomon himself.

Struggle, challenge, and change are at the core of our wisdom perspective. Wisdom sources show us that struggle and even crisis are fertile ground for growth in wisdom. We bring the stories of five Hebrew Bible characters to generate dialogue about the intersection of wisdom, work, and life. These characters faithfully struggle with life issues such as accomplishing tasks, serving as a leader, and dealing with tensions within their personal relationships. Many times, the primary struggle is between the demands of tasks and relationships; it is the same struggle we face daily in our worklife. The biblical characters, despite their own human frailties, are able to act with a sense of higher purpose in the face of major hardships or challenges, raised by themselves, by others, or by God, and ultimately grow in wisdom. And this action, based on a higher purpose, appears to be driven by a set of underlying virtues that provide building blocks for the wisdom of Solomon.

The Virtues of Our Wisdom Perspective

The virtues serve as guideposts as we undertake our search for the wisdom of Solomon. First, we consider *faith* in the story of Job. Faith is the foundation for the wisdom of Solomon. The character of Job will take us to a point of inquiring, "In what do I believe and upon what are those beliefs based?" Job introduces faithfulness as the key strand that ties together all of the biblical characters we meet. We will be challenged with the question, "What difference does belief and trust make in the biblical characters' stories and also in ours?"

Next, we encounter the virtue of *courage* in the story of David. David demonstrated an obvious kind of courage when he faced the giant warrior Goliath on the battlefield. But he also displayed a deeper courage when he faced his own mistakes and failures and attempted to lift his life and be faithful to his God. Faith and courage are introspective virtues and enable a search for wisdom within ourselves.

The virtues *compassion*, as reflected in the story of Ruth, and *integrity* and *justice*, reflected in the story of Moses, move the wisdom framework beyond a focus on self. These virtues ask us to look at other people, organizations, and the larger community. This moving outward beyond the self helps wisdom to be incorporated into the world. The enactment of wisdom in work and life and its effects are what we call Wisdom Incorporated. Wisdom becomes incorporated as we seek to develop these virtues in ourselves and enact them through our relationships and leadership. Some have recently referred to this view of leadership as "an inner path of leadership"; that is, who we are as people is as important as what we do. Seeking to become a better person—in this case, to move toward wisdom—affects the world outside of ourselves in a beneficial way.

The final virtue is *wisdom*. The story of Solomon and his great wisdom highlights the fruit of the search for wisdom. Despite the extravagance and panorama of the story, it's real value is the potential for deeper understanding and constructive action. We are better able to be in the world with an enhanced sense of authenticity, creativity, and productivity for a greater good. Aaron Feuerstein powerfully exemplified this with his faithful, courageous, compassionate, just, and wise leadership at Malden Mills.

The virtues may be viewed as interactive; each virtue builds off the other. For example, faith can establish the courage to act with compassion. And compassion is necessary for a wise understanding of justice. The virtues guide us again and again as we encounter challenge and confront the intersection of wisdom with our lives.

∞

As you take your next step, the rock beneath your foot gives way and you barely find a handhold on a jutting boulder. Steadying yourself and with a final massive heave, you throw yourself over the edge and onto the welcoming flat ground. Your focus settles on the seated figure of a white-haired old man. He looks at you and says, "Tell me, how do you see life, my child?"

The Faith of Job

THE STORY OF JOB

(Adapted from the Book of Job[12])

∞

Job was a good man, a righteous man, who tried to live as God wished him to live. Despite these positive qualities of Job, however, great misfortune suddenly appeared in his life. Almost everything he had was taken away from him.

One day when his sons and daughters were eating and drinking wine in the eldest brother's house, a messenger came to Job and said, "The oxen were plowing and the donkeys were feeding beside them, and the Sabeans fell on them and carried them off, and killed the servants with the edge of the sword; I alone have escaped to tell you."While he was still speaking, another came and said, "The fire of God fell from heaven and burned up the sheep and the servants, and consumed them; I alone have escaped to tell you." While he was still speaking another came and said, "The Chaldeans formed three columns, made a raid on the camels and carried them off, and killed the servants with the edge of the sword: I alone have escaped to tell you." While he was still speaking, another came and said, "Your sons and daughters were eating and drinking wine in their eldest brother's house, and suddenly a great wind came across the desert, struck the four corners of the house, and it fell on the young people, and they are dead; I alone have escaped to tell you." (Job 1: 13-19)

Then Job's health failed, and he became contaminated with boils all over his body from head to foot. Job lost everything, and he began to question why such bad things were happening to him. When Job's wife and friends mocked him for maintaining his loyalty to his Creator during this time of suffering, Job persevered in his faith in God:

> Naked I came from my mother's womb, and naked shall I return there; the Lord gave and the Lord has taken away; blessed be the name of the Lord. (Job 1:21)

Job struggled to make sense of how great misfortune could befall him when he had been such a righteous man. He had tried to do everything that was expected of a good, honest, and faithful man and had assumed he would receive his just rewards. Job's fundamental beliefs were shattered.

Job suffered and struggled at the very core of who he was. He struggled and came to a new understanding of himself and God. Job gained a richer, deeper set of beliefs and was blessed with great abundance, a result of his gain in wisdom.

> The Lord blessed the latter days of Job more than his beginning; and he had fourteen thousand sheep, six thousand camels, a thousand yoke of oxen, and a thousand donkeys. He also had seven sons and three daughters. . . . In all the land there were no women as beautiful as Job's daughters; and their father gave them an inheritance along with their brothers. After this, Job lived one hundred and forty years, and saw his children, his children's children, four generations. And Job died, old and full of days. (Job 42:12-17)

WHEN WE LOSE THAT WHICH IS MOST VALUABLE

∽

Historically, within organizations, there has been a natural tendency to believe that if we do the right things, as defined by the organization or the wider society—respect authority, work hard, follow directions, do our best, treat others well—then we will be rewarded with positive outcomes and certainly not be punished with negative ones. This is sometimes referred to as the "old-school mentality." It is a way of thinking that has supported and nourished hierarchies and bureaucracies over the decades, and even societal order over the centuries.

The term *old-school* is particularly apropos language for this essay, since we are addressing one of the oldest and most challenging stories in the ancient literature. It is a story that confronts most conventional logic on how to get ahead in our work and life. It is particularly fitting as we begin to consider how biblical teachings from ancient times can be fresh and relevant for today. The rich challenge this relatively short book in the Old Testament raises again and again throughout our lives is nicely captured in this descriptive narrative about an earlier encounter of one of our authors with the book of Job.

> I first encountered the story of Job in an undergraduate comparative literature seminar at Michigan State University over twenty-five years ago. I remember that I felt uncomfortable carrying around the Bible that served as one of our textbooks.

I joined other juniors and seniors who tried to sort out what it meant to "lose it all" before we had yet, in our own lives, gained some sense of "having it." We engaged the story at a fairly superficial level of characters and plot; it seemed so removed from my life.

Ironically, I have returned to that story at a different place and time. A lifetime, it seems, has passed by. Marriage, graduate school, raising children, jobs and careers, cross-country moves, lots of "it." And, through it all, struggling with the conditions of life and where I found myself. Trying to find some grounding in new places and trying to make sense of new territory. Trying to live a life out of all that's been held up as good and right.

But a time comes when we meet the unexpected, something that is beyond our notion of how life is and beyond our capacity to explain. A marriage fails; a company files bankruptcy or downsizes and we find ourselves without a career track, a key role to play, or a paycheck; our children betray us, our bodies betray us, the system betrays us. "This isn't the way it is supposed to be!" we cry in despair. We may find ourselves *living* the story of Job.

The story of Job centers on belief. In fact it addresses the very deeply held beliefs upon which we experience and interpret life. Beliefs are formed from what we experience, observe, are taught, remember, and feel. That is, we form these inner foundational structures largely from the perceptions of the world that we accumulate throughout our lives. Our beliefs craft who we are, how we see other people, what we do, and how and why we do what we do.

All seems well and good as long as our continued life experiences conform to the expectations we hold based on our beliefs. Thus, the beliefs we hold are largely contingent on our life conditions. For Job, as for most of us, there seems to be a thin line between living life comfortably "in the groove" and getting into a rut. Presumably, if the world continues to conform to our beliefs and we find a comfortable way to proceed in our work and lives, then we will likely continue to function the way we have in the past. We get into a daily routine, make the same kinds of choices as before, and avoid troubling challenges that may call into question our mode of living.

However, when life doesn't conform to our beliefs, then things begin to go awry. When conditions change, our beliefs become vulnerable and possibly fractured. An uncomfortable feeling develops that something is not right and we seek ways to make sense of it. Some times, as in the case of Job, extreme changes can drive us to examine ultimate life issues. Since life is no longer fitting our belief-based expectations, our sense of truth is capsized. When we are faced with altered, even life-shattering conditions, we are forced to call our beliefs, our basis for truth, into question. Job called into question not only himself but also God. God was the basis of Job's beliefs about what he was supposed to do in life and He affected Job's understanding of who he was (a "righteous man").

We have learned through countless studies that change is one of the most resisted aspects of working and living. People are generally defensive about any kind of change that will affect them directly. Many authors have written about a variety of strategies for overcoming resistance to, and managing, change. Of all the challenges we face, perhaps there is no greater threat than the forces that push us to reexamine our most fundamental beliefs and to face the possibility of change at the core of our being. It may well be that it is our fundamental beliefs that we hold most valuable.

"Being challenged about something we do," and "a crisis about who we are," can represent the ends of a continuum of life challenges. However, when all that we do defines who we are, we may find ourselves confronting a crisis like Job. Job is a righteous man who tries to do what is right and expected by God. Job and others view him as righteous as long as his life is going well, as long as he is healthy, wealthy, and has a contented family.

When tragedy strikes, however, Job finds himself in pain and despair. Although his friends come to him for support and to share in his misery, one by one they begin to question his righteousness. Perhaps he was not so good after all. Why else would God punish him so harshly? Eliphaz asserts, "Is it any pleasure to the Almighty if you are righteous, or is it gain to Him if you make your ways blameless? . . . Is not your wickedness great? There is no end to your iniquities" (Job 22:3,5). And Eliphaz begins a laundry list of charges against Job, including withholding food from the hungry and sending widows away emptyhanded.

Job began to confront the issue of how he had lived, the conditions of his life, and the loss brought about by the devastation of his family and possessions. It was the heavy losses of family, possessions, status, health, and security that brought Job to a precipice. The precipice consisted of facing who he was and what his life was about, especially in relation to his understanding of God, the foundation of his major beliefs.

Upon what did he place his deepest trust and confidence in life? That he would be rewarded for doing the right things? That he could maintain a sense of competence and satisfaction aligned with always doing the right thing? That God would not fail him? His perspective on life, and the events that were forcing him to change, represented his greatest challenge. He was held captive by his perspective. *Job possessed an old-school view that righteous behavior should result in comfort, wealth, and the so-called good things of life.*

This is where we encounter another, perhaps even deeper, challenge to our life journey. It has to do with identifying what qualifies for inclusion in the categories of the good and the bad things in life, that is, what is to be welcomed and what is to be avoided. This issue is raised poignantly by the Academy Award-winning movie *American Beauty*. The movie mixes a kind of satirical view with tragic aspects of what one would think should be, at least on the surface, a comfortable modern life for a suburban American family. Throughout the film, many of the darker aspects of life—death, struggle, and loss—are held up and examined for the potential beauty they contain. Normally, of course, we look for beauty in the light, celebratory, life-filled features of the world. To discover good, even beauty, in what on the surface seems like suffering and tragedy is indeed a difficult task.

Job and his friends could only see good in the comfort and the light of the world, but darkness, challenge, and suffering are part of life too. In fact, natural laws teach us that when organisms have no challenge, no strain, they can atrophy, decline, and ultimately die. This is not to say that the message of Job is to seek out hardship and suffering, but that it will come, whether we invite it or not, and it is how we deal with it that can determine the quality of our lives.

Challenge and struggle often plant the seeds for personal growth. Consider some simple relationships between what appear to be negative and the positive outcomes they can foster: personal conflicts can lead to more mature and developed relationships; problems can lead to creative solutions and innovation; endings can pave the way for new beginnings; loss of fame or property can lead to simpler, less stressful lives; the death of organisms provides the food and nourishment for others to live; challenge leads to growth; the list goes on and on.

This kind of thinking calls us to consider changing at our very core, wherein lie the beliefs on which our lives rest. In this sense, the story of Job is but a symbol of life's paradoxes. Life has a way of trying to keep us alive by continually shifting, sometimes ever so slightly and other times quite dramatically, our understanding, which may include the ideas we hold as ultimate truths. It may be that when we do the right things life sometimes rewards us, not with comfort and prosperity, but with conditions that challenge and cause us to grow even more.

In order to fully embrace and benefit from this potential of life, we must face head-on the whole issue of change. A favorite story involves an outspoken employee in a company that had long operated using a traditional organizational structure, where supervisors closely monitored and controlled workers. A decision had been made to implement team-based worker empowerment in his work area, which included the removal of the supervisors. The intent was to free up workers to make more choices and have more say in the operation, and one anticipated outcome of this change was that they would enjoy increased feelings of importance and meaning in their work. When the worker was informed of all this, however, he responded by slamming his fist on a table, stating "I demand my right to have a supervisor to tell me what to do!" Clearly, this worker's beliefs about how organizations should operate constrained him from even considering the possibility that there might be some benefits if things were done differently.

Like this worker, we each confront a set of choices when we encounter changing circumstances. We can uphold our belief. We can argue, fight, or try to discount or destroy the challenger. Job faced a series of challengers and had varying responses based on his strict adherence to his belief about himself as a righteous man. When his friends and wife challenged his character, he discounted them. He held stringently to the claim that he had always done what was right. He challenged and argued with God, questioning God's righteousness in light of his sense of his own innocence. And, throughout these dialogues, Job struggled with his own sense of hope and worth: "I loathe my life: I will give free utterance to my complaint; I will speak in the bitterness of my soul. . . My spirit is broken, my days are extinct, the grave is ready for me" (Job 10:1; 17:1). He was sacrificing his own sense of worth at the cost of maintaining his belief in being right.

When we hold fast, as Job did, to this kind of righteous thinking we miss the point. Life is not really about being comfortable, without challenge or hardship. Rather, the essence of life expressed by the story of Job seems to say we must encounter the whole experience, the easy and joyous and the difficult and tragic. We are challenged to transcend the simple thinking that when we do "right" we will enjoy only the light and sweet aspects of life. We are challenged to see the seeds of our fullest living in the difficult soil of our life experiences, and we are challenged to see the beauty that can come out of the darkness. This brings us to the threshold of a most powerful virtue we call faith. Faith can equip us to cope and thrive in the face of those difficult aspects of life that, as with Job and his friends, we don't understand.

WHAT SUSTAINS US?

∞

So far, we have approached the book of Job at the basic level of belief in the logical connection between righteous doing and receiving positive blessings in life. That is, there seems to be an inherent challenge in the human condition to move beyond the basic thinking that, if we make the "right choices" and do the "right things," then we will be blessed with comfort and prosperity.

A lengthy article appeared in a major city newspaper recently that discussed the tendency of many wealthy people to cling to beliefs and practices about frugality that they have held all their lives, even though these beliefs no longer make sense in their current life circumstances. Stories of well-off, middle-aged professionals moving heavy appliances at risk of life and limb, or spending their limited personal and family weekend time on extensive lawn and home-repair work to avoid hiring someone at nominal cost, were presented in the article.[13] A common explanation by those interviewed was that they were brought up with certain values about thriftiness and that they were not going to throw money away on something they could do for themselves.

We do have a choice whether to rely on long-held beliefs despite changes in our life conditions or to open to a new understanding growing out of the changing conditions. Sometimes this potential new knowledge calls on us to look beyond our current thinking and earlier understanding.

This is particularly true as we embark on the new millennium. Technology and globalism have brought us face to face with a transformative time where creativity and personal responsibility are sorely needed. We are called to meet this challenge by marching into a most feared place: the unknown. Change is moving at hyperspeed, and interconnectedness, across cultures and through ever-advancing technologies, has vastly increased the complexity of life on our planet.

All this means we must somehow absorb the fact that there are aspects of life we can neither predict nor explain, but that are just as much a part of life as the ones more dependable and predictable. That is, we can take faith and have courage to face our limits of knowing and take a step into what is unknown to us. After Job extinguished all of his arguments and searched the full boundaries of his beliefs about himself as a righteous man and how he understood God in relation to that, he found himself at a dead end. He realized that there was more beyond what he knew, much more.

This was a major transitional step for Job. He finally opened to understanding himself and God differently, more deeply. In the process he began to grow in wisdom. "Who is this that hides counsel without knowledge? Therefore I have uttered what I did not understand, things too wonderful for me, which I did not know. 'Hear and I will speak: I will question you, and you declare to me.' I had heard of you by the hearing of the ear, but now my eye sees you" (Job 42:3-5).

Ultimately, the struggle centers on the issue of faith. Do we possess faith? If so, in what do we have faith?

Faith is the first virtue we encounter in this book on the pathway to gaining wisdom and incorporating it into our lives and our work. Faith is the foundation for our challenging but worthwhile journey. Without faith we will shrink and retreat from challenge and struggle. And, when we are not challenged, we will simply continue to do business as usual, whether it is effective or not. That is, we will not stray from the well-worn path because we do not want to face challenge or struggle. We will avoid taking risks because we lack the belief that we can face the potential difficulties they can pose.

Similarly, when our faith is in strictly traditional business values, we will adopt traditional business approaches. We will pay close attention to the numbers and follow strategies that have been used many times before. We will do business as usual. Unfortunately, as the world continues to change at an accelerating rate and the climate for business becomes more and more complex and competitive, doing business as usual is simply not enough. In fact, doing business as usual will likely lead to failure in an increasing number of cases.

In addition, operating from a position of little or no faith can lead to an unsatisfied and purposeless existence. Faith in a greater spiritual force for good, for example, can enable us to take the steps to reexamine our beliefs and behaviors. And faith provides a foundation for stepping into the world for the benefit of others—an idea we will continue to examine in this book.

Without faith, meaningful incorporation of valuable virtues, and, ultimately, wisdom, will be blocked. Faith provides the impetus for making the hard choices and facing the difficult challenges that can stretch us and help us to grow. It empowers us to face life and move toward wisdom, as did Job.

But wisdom is not the end of the journey. It is not some proverbial pot of gold at the end of the rainbow. Wisdom is continually cultivated as we encounter life, particularly the parts of life that challenge and even wound us. Just as a bone heals so that it is strongest at the point of a previous fracture, our growth and wisdom can become most abundant where we constructively meet and learn from hardship and challenge.

Furthermore, wisdom is not simply a symbolic reward for having successfully met the challenges of life. Rather, wisdom is something that can be immeasurably useful as we continue our life journey. In fact, perhaps the best way to characterize what it is to be wise is to gain an understanding of what wisdom is and how to apply it to life. This is a timely insight because the opportunities for impacting a new way of learning, working, and living have never been greater. We are in the early stages of an era of unprecedented progress in powerfully useful areas such as science, technology, and health care. If we are able to grow equally in wisdom there can be a very promising future for humankind.

So where and how can we encounter and obtain wisdom? We encounter it as we face new difficulties and challenges during our continuing journey into the unknown. And the key to this uncertain journey is faith, a belief and trust in a greater good beyond ourselves. Job eventually had to let go of long-held beliefs that no longer applied or worked for his life. This letting go created space for new belief in forces beyond his earlier understanding and, ultimately, for faith to undergird his life into the unknown future. In our life and work we are challenged to do the same.

The Courage of David

THE STORY OF DAVID

(Adapted from I and II Samuel; I Kings: 1-2)

∞

David was the great grandson of Ruth and the youngest of eight brothers. As a youth, David looked over his father's sheep, and he displayed his fidelity and courage in this capacity by slaying both a lion and a bear.

David was very talented musically; he was a master of the lyre and later composed psalms. David was called to the court of Saul, the first king of Israel, to play his harp and soothe the king when he was troubled by an evil spirit.

David first gained public recognition as a result of his battle with Goliath (I Samuel 17: 1-58). In this classic story, the Philistines marshalled their armies and drove the children of Israel away from their homes. Saul, the king of Israel, gathered his armies to confront the Philistines. However, Saul and his men could do nothing. They were paralyzed by the sight of the Philistine leader, Goliath, who was a giant. No one wanted to confront the giant; everyone was afraid of Goliath.

David could not believe that all of the men were afraid to fight Goliath, so he volunteered to do battle with the giant Philistine. King Saul replied, "You are not able to go against this Philistine. . . for you are just a boy, and he has been a warrior from his youth" (I Samuel 17:33). But David told Saul that his experience with killing lions and bears to protect his sheep, plus his faith in God, would help him to vanquish the giant. David convinced Saul that nothing could deter him, so Saul gave David his blessing to fight Goliath.

David put his hand in his bag, took out a stone, slung it, and struck the Philistine on his forehead; the stone sank into his forehead, and he fell face down on the ground. (I Samuel 17: 49)

The military fame that David gained as a result of his victory over Goliath, David's marriage to Saul's daughter, and David's friendship with Jonathan (Saul's son) made Saul jealous of David. In fact, Saul tried to kill David. David was forced to flee for his life, and he became the head of a group of warriors. David was able to avoid Saul's attempts to capture him, and he magnanimously spared Saul's life when the opportunity later arose to kill him. David felt that killing Saul would go against God's will. Soon thereafter, Saul died.

The Lord said to David, "Go up. . . to Hebron" (II Samuel 2:1). David did so and was selected to be king of Judah in Hebron, where he reigned for seven years. David inherited a broken country fraught with infighting, yet as king he was able to restore peace. David was a king of all the people, not just his loyal followers, and because of his strong leadership the rest of Israel made him their king. The reign of David lasted for nearly thirty-three years.

God had found great favor in David, and David was faithful to God. But David was human, and subject to temptations. His most noted failing was his adultery with Bathsheba, a beautiful married woman. When Bathsheba found herself pregnant, David ordered her husband's death on the battlefield so he could have her as his wife (II Samuel:11).

Because of David's great sin, the Lord struck the child at birth, and it died. David acknowledged his sin before God.

Soon thereafter a second child was born, a boy who would grow up to be the great King Solomon.

David's reign was full of military battles. Fighting occurred even within his own family over who would succeed him. Ultimately, when David was an old man, he had Solomon anointed as his successor, saying "Be strong, be courageous, and keep the charge of the Lord your God, walking in his ways. . . so that you may prosper in all that you do and wherever you turn" (I Kings: 2:2-3). David died shortly thereafter and was buried in the City of David.

WHEN WE ARE FACE TO FACE WITH FEAR OR THREAT

∞

As in biblical times when David mustered the courage to battle Goliath, courage continues to be a virtue that is at the core of the human spirit. It is defined as bravery, fearlessness, confidence, or, more colloquially, as "having the guts" to persist in the face of threat or danger. To be viewed as courageous is one of the most powerful compliments a person can receive.

Acts of courage are often accompanied by medals in war, recognition in the community, and respect among friends and family. Courage, unlike wealth, prestige, and status, cannot be bought or accumulated. It is more like respect and honor, attributes bestowed upon you through the perceptions of others. Courage sets in motion a delicate process in which people honor your actions, respect your motives, and appreciate your humility. So delicate is this, that to call yourselves courageous might change how others see you. For David, courage was always based on his faith in his God. It was a belief in something greater than himself that gave him the confidence to overcome his fears.

Forms of Courage

As a basic human virtue that plays an essential role on the journey to living and leading with wisdom, courage is the engine that pushes us beyond our safety zones to encounter the challenges we have not yet mastered and, sometimes, ones we haven't anticipated. The call for courage is heard throughout our lifetime. It is only the challenges that differ.

Youthful Courage

As a boy who was somewhat closer in stature to David than Goliath, I remember the smarter, more agile, warrior's victory over the gargantuan Goliath as one of my favorite Sunday School stories. To be honest, I did not think much about faith in those days. This was a win for the good guy, the underdog! Perhaps I was not ready at the time to question the source of this courage more deeply.

Now, as a parent, I watch my children face their Goliaths with their own brand of youthful courage. My young son steels himself to sleep without his pacifier by lining up his favorite stuffed animals, eyeing the sliced-apple treat (to take the place of the soothing "binky"), and asking for a back rub and a story to help him calmly drift into his dreams. My youngest daughter faces the congregation as she fearlessly chants her Bat Mitzvah passage. Years of learning the Hebrew language and months of tutoring by a beloved Cantor have helped reduce the risk of disaster as she sings out the ancient melodies to appreciative congregants, relatives, and friends.

I cannot help daydreaming for a moment about the courage that I had to summon in my thirteenth year to participate in this timeless rite of passage. I could feel the tears of pride welling up as my focus returned to my daughter; she sang the closing prayers and smiled with confidence and relief as her portion of the Sabbath service came to an end. Soon she would be at her party, among her friends and family, enjoying the celebration of her transition from youth to adulthood in the Jewish faith. It seemed at that moment that the wisdom of this ritual not only solidified my daughter's spiritual faith but also strengthened and renewed mine. A generation from now, her child would stand before the congregation and the cycle would repeat itself, as it has in our religion for over 2000 years.

My oldest daughter is an athlete. As she stands on the starting blocks, coiled to dive into the pool at the sound of the starter's horn, I sit in the gallery, my thumb poised to start the stopwatch that will measure her performance. She has progressed from a young girl, racing with abandon against evermore-difficult opponents, to a seasoned competitor, spurred on by her own demanding standards for continual improvement. She has also evolved into a leader, able to see beyond the score and to focus on the goals and dreams of her teammates.

Forced to sit out her final high-school championship meet because of an illness, she had the courage to throw her available energy into cutting fish shapes out of colored paper for each of her teammates. Everyone on the team received a personal fish with customized decorations and words of encouragement. She could not hide the tears when she could only be a spectator at races she had won for her school the previous year, but her fish told me she had started the transition from youthful courage to a form of courage that seemed a step closer to wisdom. I knew that she was preparing herself for the increasingly demanding calls for courage in the years to come.

The Courage to Respond
When Things Knock You Down

For many of us, to look back at the courage of our youth or the entrepreneurial adventures early in our career brings a smile to our face. The immortality we feel in our youth, and our resiliency from an occasional setback in a flurry of business and personal adventures, represent heady times. For many, faith in ourselves, the economy, and the future were enough to maintain our momentum.

Now, events in our lives and the lives of others around us suddenly challenge us to step up and revisit the meaning of courage. A colleague approached me recently with these words: "Tomorrow, I begin my radiation treatment." I had known of his health concerns. As he continued to relate to me the possible side effects of his treatments, the course of his therapies, his hopes for a favorable outcome, and his realization that there are no guarantees, I recognized that he was summoning up a form of courage that was hard for me to fathom.

A line from an old Bruce Springsteen song "When You're Along" played over and over in my head.[14] "But there's things that'll knock you down you don't even see coming." The next line of the song, "and send you crawling like a baby back home," rang so true for me.

My best friend from my youth had suffered a disabling stroke. He could no longer work in his medical specialty. Another acquaintance was fired prematurely because of downsizing. He was devastated. The death of my own beloved father resulted in a void I thought could never be filled.

Watching my friend lose his good health, my acquaintance lose his secure and rewarding job, and my father lose his life made me aware of the courage each of them was forced to summon in order to cope with these crises. My friend had an incredible spirit as he faced endless hours of rehabilitation. My acquaintance had to redefine who he was without the corporate title. Shaken by what had happened, he was able to overcome the humiliation of not being able to pay all of his bills and move on to work that was less lucrative but in many ways more satisfying.

In the last months of his life, my father was able to face his death with dignity and peace. I knew that his courage came from the same faith that had helped him face the loss of his family to the horrors of the Nazi concentration camps. Yet he was able to emigrate to the United States, find the love of his life, and create a family whom he taught to honor the lessons of the past and to believe in the potential goodness of the future. His life having been spared, he counted every day as a gift from God.

Experiencing these powerful events in a rather short period of time increased my sense of vulnerability and left me with hard questions regarding my own mortality and my legacy to my family, friends, and colleagues. I realized that what had been thrust on my loved ones without warning could paradoxically serve as a wakeup call for me to explore more fully what was meaningful in my life.

Did I have the courage to break down the walls of my comfort zone and strengthen the connection between my spiritual values and my daily behavior, at work and at home? For nearly everyone, health, job, and family challenges are only a heartbeat away. It seemed clear that my concerns went beyond financial matters but dealt with the human spirit. I did not have to wait for my own health or job crisis to occur before I embarked on the path of wisdom.

Once I realized this, it was easier than I expected to begin to make changes. When a student visited during my office hours, instead of asking "What can I do for you?" I began to ask "What is your dream?" My office hours have never been so productive.

The Courage of Spiritual Wisdom

For some, the courage to challenge the conventional wisdom of the times was a part of a long and deep attachment to a set of spiritual virtues. For Aaron Feuerstein, the owner of Malden Mills, the values of business were only part of his business philosophy. An important goal in his life was an idea of oneness, whereby he practiced reconciling the teachings of his spiritual source, Judaism, with his daily interactions with employees in his textile factory. He had always treated his employees with respect and kindness, and he paid above-average salaries. His efforts enabled him to see a simple truth. That is, bringing his spiritual values to work could bring out the best in his employees because they believed that Feuerstein worked at finding the best within himself.

Part of his task as a successful businessman was to develop an advocacy relationship with his employees. The motivation and loyalty of his employees, so essential to producing a high-quality product, were not negotiable in a union contract. It had to be communicated daily from the heart. Thus when he nearly lost everything in the tragic fire at his mill, Feuerstein's ability to reconcile the values of his business with his spiritual virtues of courage and faith had already created the bond that led to the superhuman efforts of his employees to save the business and ultimately benefit everyone involved. His legacy was to extend well beyond the burnt-out mill in Massachusetts. It would ignite a spark in the hearts of many businesspeople who needed just such a role model to help them access their own acts of courage.

For those of us hoping to raise our "spiritual intelligence," the story of David serves as a helpful guide. It is, perhaps, his fallibility that makes him most endearing to us. As you will see in subsequent stories, David's adulterous affair with the beautiful Bathsheba was an outrageous abuse of power that would rival any modern-day political scandal.

But David struggles onward through these detours on the way to wisdom, as must we all. It is his ongoing faith in his God, and his tendency to act out of his heart that give him the courage to learn from his mistakes and overcome fear and threat in its many forms. David's fallibility, his faith, and his heart can be guiding principles as we explore the various facets of courage in our quest to reconcile business values and spiritual virtues on the journey toward living and leading with the wisdom of Solomon.

WHEN WE HAVE TO CHALLENGE
GREAT POWER

∾

Working with the wisdom of Solomon does not happen without life experiences to draw upon. Perhaps no biblical character can claim a richer variety of life experiences than the father of Solomon, King David. At first glance, David seems like an appropriate role model for today's business leaders. He challenged the conventional wisdom of his day by outsmarting his much-larger opponent, Goliath the Philistine, with speed, ingenuity, and surprise. Recognizing that he could not compete with Goliath in strength or size, David prepared for his confrontation by the counter-intuitive act of removing his bronze helmet and coat of mail. Freed from his heavy armaments, he was able to access the speed and flexibility he had relied upon when protecting his sheep from dangerous predators. When David appeared, carrying only his shepherd's staff, Goliath mocked him, shouting "Am I a dog, that you come to me with sticks?"

Goliath, the challenger, the symbol of conventional wisdom that the strongest and mightiest wins, had boasted, "Choose a man for yourselves . . . if he is able to fight with me and kill me, then we will be your servants; but if I prevail against him and kill him, then you shall be our servants and serve us" (I Samuel 17:8-9).

David responded with courage. Moments later Goliath lay dead, felled by a stone launched from David's slingshot. David had a vision of what he must do to face the challenge of Goliath. He was armed with a belief in something beyond himself, a belief that God would protect him. He drew from his experience as a shepherd where he had to protect his flock from wild animals. Thus, he felt confident that he could bring down Goliath.

What makes this one of the Bible's most often-told stories is the triumph of good over evil, of the underdog over the favored, of mind over muscle. What makes it so appealing is the simplicity of the challenge, the swiftness of the confrontation, and the successful outcome of the battle.

When Goliath announced the terms of battle, pledging that the losers would serve as servants to the winners, he set up far-reaching and immediate consequences for a single encounter. This is how we would all like to do battle with our Goliaths.

Business leaders continually face the Goliaths of bureaucratic resistance to change, the allure of short-term gain, and company politics when they try to summon up the courage to revitalize their organizations. Ordinary employees, according to researchers, often come up with the most creative ideas for improving productivity, but unless the company they work for supports challenges to the conventional wisdom, the most imaginative contributions are often left on the drawingboard.[15]

For those who challenge conventional wisdom in their field, the process is seldom simple, swift, and successful. What looks like a sudden breakthrough is often the culmination of years of preparation and training, learning difficult lessons through entrepreneurial failures, and finally hitting the right combination after countless negative results in the "laboratory." Many of those who have challenged the conventional wisdom in their field have had a vision of a new way to solve problems, faith in their ideas, and the resolve to answer their critics.

The Courage to Challenge
Conventional Wisdom

In 1994 Barry Marshall, a doctor in the Australian outback, had only his faith in his own medical observations to fight the formidable resistance of his profession.[16] The ordeal he experienced at the hands of his colleagues and the leading pharmaceutical firms was neither simple nor brief. In 1994 he made a discovery that would make medical history: ulcers are caused by the bacterium *H. Pylori*, and can be cured by antibiotic medication. His observations completely contradicted conventional medical wisdom. Until his observations were verified in 1995, the medical establishment believed that ulcers were caused by stomach acid, brought about by spicy foods and stress. A bland diet and stress management were the primary treatment methods. There was no cure. For the stomach acid that remained, treatment of the symptoms through a daily regimen of acid-reducing medication was prescribed.

Pharmaceutical firms were enjoying windfall profits of over $4 billion annually from prescription medications such as Tagamet and Zantac and over-the-counter palliatives such as Mylanta. Four million ulcer patients in the United States alone were spending over $100 per month to combat the painful symptoms of ulcers.[17] The healthcare industry profited from costly medical examinations, follow-up visits, and diagnostic tests, and there was no cure in sight. Barry Marshall was a physician from a rural area of Australia, one of the most isolated countries of the world. In contrast to the sophisticated research laboratories of Europe and North America, Dr. Marshall's claims were based on his personal observations of several patients. It is no wonder that Marshall's pronouncement was viewed with skepticism by the medical establishment.

Marshall began to realize the magnitude of the Goliath he faced: the size, credibility, and power of the medical establishment allied with the pharmaceutical firms. However, armed with faith in his observations and the courage to stay the course, he endured rejection of his scientific papers at prestigious conferences and ridicule of his audacity to challenge the entire medical profession. "Who is this guy?" questioned one confrontational member of the scientific community.[18] But Marshall was undaunted, determined to put his observations to the test and silence his critics. He resorted to a dramatic demonstration of faith in his findings. Not unlike other memorable medical pioneers, he infected himself with *H. pylori*. While he had hoped to develop an ulcer himself, and then cure it with antibiotics, he became acutely ill soon after the experiment began and was forced to take antibiotics before he could develop an ulcer. Nevertheless, after recovering from his illness he was ready to try his antibiotic treatment of ulcer patients on a larger scale.

The results were sensational! Eighty percent of the ulcer patients were cured forever with a regimen of commonly used medication that took less than one month to administer and cost no more than $300. Barry Marshall's discovery ended the expensive and painful long-term suffering of most ulcer patients. The mighty medical establishment is now in the process of rewriting the textbooks, fully embracing what they had ridiculed only a few years ago. The pharmaceutical manufacturers, trying to make the most of a significant loss, turned matters over to their marketing departments. The results are highly visible in the media and print advertisements, where medications such as Tagamet and Zantac are reborn with the slogan "now for heartburn."

The Courage to Make a Difference for Others

Like many heroes of their day, Barry Marshall had enough faith in his observations to pursue them until his curiosity about their validity was satisfied. The pursuit of truth often faces many obstacles. For Moses, it was forty years of wandering before reaching the promised land; for Nelson Mandela, it was twenty-seven years in prison before presiding over the end of apartheid in South Africa. What these leaders share is a common mindset that enabled them to face danger and uncertainty with confidence and resolve.

All of them struggled with the complexity of their circumstances, yet they sustained a clear vision of the road they must travel. They faced the reality that reaching the promised land (freedom from disease, social peace and harmony) is rarely accomplished by a single act of bravery. In our work and life, the complexities and the long duration of Barry Marshall's heroic journey strike a familiar chord. Each day requires the courage to face our Goliaths, dealing with unethical business practices, outdated bureaucracy, unpredictable markets, management/union conflict, and legal challenges.

The story of David and Goliath and that of Barry Marshall depict a form of courage that confronts an enormous challenge with a combination of experience and faith. David's experience as a protector of his sheep, along with his faith in God's support, enabled him to challenge conventional wisdom and defeat a much larger opponent. Dr. Marshall trusted his medical experience and had faith in the veracity of his observations. When he challenged the conventional wisdom of the medical profession with his unusual findings, the path to gaining their eventual acceptance was neither simple nor swift (as in David's case), but the final outcome was successful.

David, Dr. Marshall, and those who, like Nelson Mandela, struggle for social justice and succeed, have made a difference not only in their own lives but also for countless others. The Israelites were kept from slavery, ulcer patients no longer suffer needless debilitating pain, and black South Africans have moved beyond the dehumanization of apartheid because *someone* had the courage to make a difference.

WHEN WE ULTIMATELY MUST FACE OURSELVES

∞

David was a born leader with a strong faith. Tales of his adolescence and young adulthood read like a resume of courageous acts, creative accomplishments, and compassionate decisions. He eagerly accepted the challenge of confronting Goliath, and overpowered him with a carefully thought out attack.

The haunting melodies of the Psalms composed by David served as an ancient version of an antidepressant for the dark moods of King Saul. And, some years later, after a failed attempt by King Saul to have David killed, David was also able to summon his compassion and his faith and spare the life of Saul.

And yet, despite these admirable attributes, it is perhaps from David's human failings that we learn the most important lessons for living wisely in today's complex world. Like many other heroes of the Bible, David was soon to reveal a darker side of his personality. He would engage in such a deliberate act of impaired moral judgment that it would change his life and the destiny of his kingdom forever.

Soon after David became King of all Israel, he was tempted by the sight of a beautiful woman bathing in her dwelling across from his palace.

It happened, late one afternoon, when David rose from his couch and was walking about on the roof of the king's house, that he saw from the roof a woman bathing; the woman was very beautiful. David sent someone to inquire about the woman. It was reported, "This is Bathsheba daughter of Eliam, the wife of Uriah the Hittite." So David sent messengers to get her, and she came to him, and he lay with her. Then she returned to her house. The woman conceived; and she sent and told David, "I am pregnant." (II Samuel 11:2-5)

To add insult to injury, David later arranged to have Uriah, Bathsheba's husband, killed. This is supported by David's orders to one of his servants:

Set Uriah in the forefront of the hardest fighting, and then draw back from him, so that he may be struck down and die. (II Samuel 11:15)

This story of David's lust for Bathsheba, his adultery with her, and his subsequent murder of Uriah depicts David as a flawed human being who gave in to his basest desires and showed little awareness or remorse regarding the commandments he was breaking.

"What was he thinking?" we ask. This man who exemplified faith and courage suddenly behaves completely in his own self-interest, seeming unconcerned about the damage his impulsive actions would have on others.

The circuitous path to wisdom pauses at many stops along the way to ask "Why do we do what we do?" Here David seems a prisoner of his desires and completely devoid of what we have been calling courage. This story has a familiar ring to it. Countless leaders, from the biblical era to contemporary times, have succumbed to similar temptations.

The Hebrew Bible suggests that, to a large degree, each of us must take responsibility for our own actions. However, social psychologists have learned that the cultural context can significantly influence how we behave. People who are ordinarily caring toward others can temporarily lose sight of their values when placed in a situation where competition and success are the prevailing values.[19]

Playing the Game

In the competitive culture of global business there is tremendous pressure continually to improve return on investment, quarterly earnings, and the market price of a stock. It is not surprising that the behaviors that contribute to the growth and happiness of family and friendships may differ from the behaviors that seem necessary to "take care of business." Just as the Cosa Nostra created two separate codes of conduct, one for family members and one for work, we may find ourselves vulnerable to similar temptations. This phenomenon of human behavior has been replayed hundreds of times in a remarkable exercise, "Circles, Squares, and Triangles," that I include in many of my graduate MBA classes and professional seminars.[20]

In this activity participants are randomly divided into three groups. The random aspect of their grouping is important, as will be seen later. The stated purpose of the exercise is to practice negotiation skills by requiring participants to trade colored chips (each color has a different point value) that they have received in an envelope at the start of the exercise. By trading wisely and accumulating more chips of the same color, participants can obtain bonuses and improve their total points.

However, without the traders' knowledge, the exercise is designed to favor one of the groups so they get richer. The game design discriminates against another group so that it continually gets poorer, and the third group stays at about the same level of points per round as at the beginning. Near the end of the exercise, the "rich group" is rewarded for its trading success by being allowed to make the rules for the final round. During the twenty minutes allotted for setting the rules of the final round, the two remaining groups are invited to recommend, in writing, rule changes. The rich group may then do whatever it wishes with the written recommendations.

Even though the exercise is portrayed as a competitive negotiation exercise, the true goal is to examine the differences in behavior among those participants in the group who are continually becoming richer and another group that does poorly and has no chance of improvement.

In hundreds of administrations of this exercise over the years, the results have been the same. The participants in the successful group are animated, sitting close together, working hard to develop a set of trading rules that will consolidate their wealth and provide only token opportunities, or none at all, for the lesser groups to improve their situations. Written suggestions submitted by the other groups are typically rejected, and it is not uncommon to see members of the rich group read these suggestions, laugh at them, crumple the page into a ball, and toss them into a wastebasket or onto the floor.

Meanwhile the losing group's behavior is equally predictable, manifested as apathy, grim faces, disinterest in the exercise, requests to be excused to the rest room and, at times, engagement in dishonest actions such as stealing chips that are deliberately left out at the front of the room for precisely that purpose. There are many other details of this exercise, but suffice it to say the predictability of behaviors of the haves and the have-nots is chilling.

What is most important is that it doesn't seem to matter which individuals are assigned to which groups. It is a context of power and success and the other context of hopelessness that has a significant impact on the behavior of people in these randomly formed groups, regardless of their individual values.

When the true purpose of the exercise is revealed during the debriefing, participants of the winning group who behave in a somewhat greedy, superior manner, report feeling guilty, ashamed, and generally embarrassed, while their hopeless counterparts express feelings of anger, deception, and manipulation.

Everyone, it seems, leaves this exercise with negative feelings, except the observers. Having been granted a reprieve from the strong cultural context of the groups mentioned, the observers are astonished at the predictability and the intensity of their peers' actions. Playing their role as dispassionate observers, it is easy for them to see that in the greedy winning group are individuals who appear to be among the most caring and compassionate individuals in the class.

Likewise, in the apathetic, hostile, losing group are some of the most productive and creative class members. From this exercise, it becomes easier to understand why well-intended individuals sometimes find it difficult to resist the social and cultural pull of a group that is trying to succeed within a strong set of rules.

If a group exercise can create a context that powerfully affects behavior in only ninety minutes, how easy it is to imagine a similar phenomenon in real work settings, which are deeply embedded in the competitive social context of our lives. Considering the cultural rules of biblical times, it may have seemed reasonable to King David, who was surrounded by advisors, soldiers, and his harem, to add one more woman to his collection and send her husband to a socially acceptable demise in battle.

Facing Yourself Squarely

The story of David and Bathsheba illustrates that we can become a prisoner of our own cultural context without realizing that the decisions being made may have significant moral costs. How do those of us who are on the "winning team," and who enjoy the game and are eager to maintain the status quo, gain the courage to face ourselves, become an observer of our culture, and gain the wisdom to do better?

To be able to view his behavior from the observer perspective, David needed help. The help came from Nathan, who was sent by the Lord. Nathan tells David a parable in which a rich man takes the lamb of a poor man. Upon hearing this story, David becomes angry, and says to Nathan "As the Lord lives, the man who did this deserves to die" (2 Samuel 12:5). Nathan replies, "You are the man," and after reciting all of the blessings (advantages) given to David, asks him why he took Uriah's wife and had him killed. To his credit, David finally sees how he has abused his power. He says to Nathan, "I have sinned against the Lord" (2 Samuel 12:13). David faced up to his actions, endured the forthcoming punishments meted out by the Lord, and began to view his actions with greater reflection through the eyes of one who now sees.

Biblical scholarship indicates that David's kingship did not begin to reach its height until after his affair with Bathsheba. As the story goes, David and Bathsheba's first son is killed by God as punishment for David's lapse in moral judgment. God also continues to create "trouble against you from within your own house" as a way of reminding David of his disregard for God's commandments.

However, in spite of his failings, David's faith in God does not waiver. David shows the courage to acknowledge his transgressions. God recognizes David's remorse for his sins and his search for a better way. Soon thereafter, Bathsheba bears their second son Solomon, an heir to the throne, who will serve the people of Israel wisely and who is chosen by God to build Israel's first holy temple.

To face oneself squarely, to behave with courage directed inwardly, can be a daunting task. For many of us there is no Nathan to appear conveniently with an appropriate parable to make sure that we "get it." Nevertheless, using the painful lessons of David to guide us, we can become better observers of our own circumstances and move a step closer to wisdom.

HOW DO WE CHOOSE
TO RESPOND?

∞

In quiet rooms, using the light of the sun by day and the soft glow of the candle by night, the hands of the ancient calligraphers inscribed the remarkable stories of David, King of Israel, onto the papyrus rolls of the Hebrew Bible. Nearly 2500 years later, technology has advanced such that the entire contents of the Bible can be transmitted anywhere in the world in a fraction of a second. And yet, the heart of meaningful human interaction remains very much the same as it did in the days of David.

We live in a different era, where wealth and power are available to more people. However, researchers have found that the pursuit of affluence and influence has not resulted in greater personal happiness than for people with more balanced life pursuits.

To dictate and accumulate may be global measures of success in a quantitative, competitive business setting, but to do so with faith, courage, compassion, integrity, justice, and wisdom, the spiritual virtues represented by our Hebrew Bible characters, is a significant challenge.

These spiritual virtues are paramount when confronting life's struggles and learning from them. The goal of living a meaningful life requires continual learning. There are times when our circumstances seem difficult or impossible and only faith is available to sustain us. What is needed for many is a moment of reflection, of taking stock and trying to latch on to what is truly important for our lives.

As our parents age and grow more dependent on us, as

our children transition through their youth, college, and join others to form their own families, as our health begins to show its vulnerabilities, and as we move into another life stage, we ask many questions of ourselves. Are we pleased with what we have become? Have we been fortunate enough to learn wisdom from our elders? Will our accumulated professional titles and financial investments be in balance with a life of meaning and giving? Did we give more than we took? What is our legacy?

Our reflection can help us to zero in on a more critical and underlying issue. Is it possible to participate in today's modern business environment by responding to the competitive system of the workplace and maintaining the collaborative vision of a spiritual life?

This is the problem that Aaron Feuerstein of Malden Mills refers to as *oneness*. "When the younger generation see business people acting one way in church and another way in business . . . they think it's phony." And yet it is easy to understand why business people behave differently in their professional and their personal lives. Any introductory course in psychology informs us that we do what we are rewarded for doing. The context of business is still conceived in our free market workplace as a competitive, survival-of-the-fittest environment. At the same time, our spiritual side emphasizes harmony, collaboration, love, and respect.

How can we reconcile these seemingly incompatible approaches to living? When you consider that incentives play an important role in work behaviors, it may seem that the spiritual virtue of courage, as depicted by David's early battlefield behavior, does little to help us reconcile the gulf between spiritual virtue and business values. However, the various ways that David embraced courage as he became a wiser person in his later years bears watching.

When one follows David to his biblical version of a mid-life crisis, where he has an affair with a beautiful young woman, we begin to see a very different form of courage. For all of his heroism in confronting great odds and winning great battles, the most difficult lessons of his life were coming to terms with himself, accepting his mistakes, and beginning to change his behavior. The incentive for contacting the inner courage necessary to face himself had to do with his private relationship to his God and his accountability to his people.

In order to engage in this private form of courage, David needed to become emotionally honest with himself and others. He needed the courage to become vulnerable. It is important to note that David was not capable of recognizing the extent of his mistakes with Bathsheba, their baby, and her husband Uriah, without the help of Nathan, who told David the parable that finally helped him recognize how his behavior had hurt others. Not only did David show the courage to look within himself for the answer, but his repentant response to Nathan signaled the courage to be vulnerable. It is often said that David lived from his heart. He was originally chosen to be King of Israel because of his ability to connect with what people were feeling.

But even a temporary hardening of his heart during his attraction to Bathsheba did not alter his basic faith. Once he recognized the error of his ways, he was able to return to a more yielding emotional state, suffer the consequences of his indiscretion, and get on with his life.

In business, vulnerability is often seen as a dysfunctional trait. Competition and performance seem to view vulnerability as a weakness that will be exploited by employees and competitors. However when we look at Aaron Feuerstein and what made this seemingly ordinary business person unique, we see his desire for oneness with his employees, to see the world through their eyes, and to earn their respect "the hard way," not through cash bonuses and superficial awards. Feuerstein consistently sought to view his factory personnel as the backbone of his business and to treat them with respect.

Aaron Feuerstein had the courage to be vulnerable and emotionally connected with his factory workers; he held the belief that *they* were the source of his business success and he engaged in behaviors that proclaimed this belief to them loud and clear.

We have seen several examples of encounters with courage. Let us explore how they may relate to your life.

Why Do We Do What We Do?

Recall the observer role in the Circles, Squares, and Triangles game. If you could play that role at work and watch yourself interacting with others, using your influence to make things happen, what would you see?

How powerful is the context of work in affecting your decisions?

How have you allowed yourself to follow the expectations of the system in which you work even though your spiritual side experiences some discomfort?

Have you ever been part of a committee or team that made a decision of inequity for women or minorities? Was it difficult for you to question the decision publicly?

Courage

What is an important act of courage that you have displayed at work?

Which kinds of courage have you embraced most easily:

youthful courage; the courage to face a great challenge; the courage to look within yourself; the courage to be open and vulnerable to your employees?

Oneness

Think of someone who you believe effectively practices the concept of "oneness."

How many of the virtues described in this book (faith, courage, compassion, integrity, a sense of fair justice, and wisdom) apply to that person?

Where is the "oneness" missing from your job?

Your Legacy

Picture yourself at a special retirement dinner in your honor. During the meal someone has put a truth serum in everyone's drink, so that after their prepared remarks they will be required to be honest about your effect on them.

What will they say?

Do you look forward to this celebration?

If not, what concerns you?

I am reminded of a prayer recited at the funeral of an amazing woman. It captures what can happen when we embrace courage:

As a drop of water in the sea, as a grain of sand on the shore are man's few days in eternity. The good things in life last for limited days, but a good name endures forever. [21]

WISDOM INC.:
INCORPORATING BUSINESS VALUES WITH SPIRITUAL VIRTUE

For this book, we chose exemplary business values that play key roles in the workplace and with which we felt the biblical characters could be identified. We have already looked within by reflecting on our beliefs and our chosen behaviors in the essays addressing Job and David. We will now shift to an outward focus by drawing upon the story of Ruth for compassionate action and service, and Moses for leadership. Ultimately, this path will bring us to the threshold of wisdom and its potential fruits in the story of Solomon.

As we continue our winding journey in search of the wisdom of Solomon, our challenge is to act according to spiritual virtues yet maintain our ability to be effective in a business sense. It is here that we encounter the classic struggle between task accomplishment and creating and maintaining a personally meaningful life that contains valued positive relationships. This is where practical and spiritual wisdom hit head on. For a poignant glimpse at this challenge, consider the spirit of the fisherman and the efficiency of the Harvard MBA in the following story.

The American businessman was at the pier of a small coastal village in South America when a small boat with just one fisherman docked. Inside the small boat were several large yellowfin tuna. The American complimented the fisherman on the quality of his fish and asked how long it took to catch them.

The fisherman replied "Only a little while." The American then asked why he didn't stay out longer and catch more fish? The fisherman said he had enough to support his family's immediate needs.

The American then asked "But what do you do with the rest of your time?"

The fisherman said, "I sleep late, fish a little, play with my children, take siesta with my wife Maria, and stroll into the village each evening, where I sip wine and play guitar with my amigos. I have a full and busy life, Señor."

The American scoffed, "I am a Harvard MBA and I can help you. You should spend more time fishing and, with the proceeds, buy a bigger boat. With the proceeds from the bigger boat you could buy several boats, and eventually you would have a fleet of fishing boats. Instead of selling your catch to a middleman you could sell directly to the processor, eventually opening your own cannery. That way, you would control the product, processing, and distribution. Then you could leave this small coastal fishing village and move to the capital city of your country, then to Los Angeles, and eventually to New York City, where you would run your expanding enterprise."

The fisherman asked, "But Señor, how long will this take?"

To which the American replied, "Fifteen to twenty years."

"But what then, Señor?"

The American laughed and said, "That's the best part. When the time is right, you would announce an IPO and sell your company stock to the public and become very rich. You would make millions!"

"Millions, Señor? Then what?"

The American said, "Then you would retire and move to a small coastal fishing village where you would sleep late, fish a little, play with your kids, take siesta with your wife, and stroll to the village in the evenings, where you could sip wine and play your guitar with your amigos."[22]

The Harvard MBA and the fisherman live in two very different worlds. The Harvard MBA is focused on practical business values and sees planning, performance, and profit as the building blocks for success. The fisherman's life is centered on living in the present, with concern for love, respect, and happiness based primarily on relationships. To some degree, each of us straddles both of these worlds. As people who work for our livelihood, we can appreciate the economic system that contributes to our well-being and has the potential to improve the standard of living for all. Yet this system, when played out with little regard for the human spirit, can resemble an efficient, well-programmed robot that lacks emotion, compassion, or joy. In fact, recent research has shown that the pursuit of affluence as a primary life goal does not result in particularly happy people. In studies across several cultures, those who choose affluence as a priority in life "tend to experience an unusual degree of anxiety and depression."[23]

The peaceful fishing village is no utopia either. Living in the present and allowing our interpersonal relationships to dominate our decision-making, works well as long as there is no disease or disaster. When the hurricane hits or the fish aren't running, the planning and resources of the Harvard MBA are just what is needed to help us weather the storm and preserve a deeply collaborative and relationship-based way of life.

For too many of us, the world of work is ruled by the values of the Harvard MBA, while we struggle to maintain the fisherman's emotional closeness with family, friends, and community. When these two worlds collide, we tend to live our lives like the double agents in Cold War films. Like the proverbial double agent, we maintain split identities, operating from two different value systems as we travel back and forth from one world to the other.

This can be exceedingly stressful as we are constantly forced to monitor which persona should appear in each situation. Behaviors for which we are rewarded in one setting may be looked at with disdain in the other. Business as usual, with its primary emphasis on financial outcomes, can rob the workplace of the enormous motivating power of the human spirit. Productivity devoid of spirit can result in a sweatshop. Where can we find help to bridge these two worlds?

It is our view that we can find the help we need from the source we have been exploring since the beginning of this book—*wisdom*. More specifically, it is the incorporating of wisdom, or what we call *Wisdom Inc.*, into our personal and work lives that can help us to move toward a healthier balance. How does Wisdom, Inc. work? Let's start with a reflective exercise where we look at a business value and a spiritual virtue and see if there is a new way they can work together. We bring our own spiritual and faith heritage, our work-life experience, and our understanding to this exercise. We move through the following steps.

Recognize

- Identify a business value and a spiritual virtue for incorporation.

- What words can you think of that describe, define, or are associated with that value and virtue?

- What feelings do the value and virtue evoke in you?

- How important is each in your work life?

Reconcile

- What relationship do you see between the value and virtue?

- What tension between the value and virtue can you identify?

- What do they have in common?

Reconstruct

- Can you see a different relationship between the value and virtue than what exists in your current work experience?

- What might that look like? You may come up with another word or idea to express the newly incorporated form of the virtue and business value.

- How can you use this new form as a guide or reference point for living and leading?

This is not a rigid process; it is a personally distinctive and powerful way we have found to help us begin incorporating wisdom into our work lives. The following example, offered by a businesswoman at a recent seminar, should help clarify how the Wisdom Inc. process can unfold.

As she read the moving story of Ruth and noted the compassion that defined her, the businesswoman immediately recognized from our list of business values that performance was a driving force in her company. It suddenly dawned on her that by combining performance, as willed by the company culture, with compassion traced to her spiritual self, she could make a connection to what she called "service." Her notion of service was characterized by high quality allied with warmth and empathy for the concerns of the employees, customers, and vendors. She recognized that she would be inspired to work with greater commitment because her spiritual needs were being tapped. Service became the rallying cry and coworkers, customers, and bosses were emboldened to think "outside of the box" and accomplish extraordinary results.

Reconciling a business value with a spiritual virtue through this kind of mental exercise can be a beginning for incorporating the wisdom process into daily work and life. Ultimately, wisdom is more fully incorporated when we are actively engaged in challenging business as usual in our dealings with our co-workers, customers, and the world at large.

The chapters that follow will focus on the relationship between a biblical character's characteristic virtue and a primary business value. The 3R process—Recognize, Reconcile,

Reconstruct—undergirded the development of the chapters. Each biblical story serves as a guide to questions that help us in our search for ways to incorporate wisdom into our work and life. Perhaps this search will reveal ways that we can personally capture the relationship-oriented wisdom of the fisherman and the practical business wisdom of the Harvard MBA.

The Compassion of Ruth

THE STORY OF RUTH

(Adapted from the Book of Ruth)

∞

Ruth was a young woman from Moab, a country whose culture was much different from that of Israel, the home of her future husband. She became the wife of an Israelite whose family had fled to Moab to escape famine in Israel. Through this marriage, Ruth became the daughter-in-law of Naomi. Another Moabite woman, Orpah, married Naomi's other son. Despite the fact that her sons married women outside the family's faith and culture, Naomi seemed to have accepted these two young women as her own daughters.

Then, tragedy struck. Both of Naomi's sons died around the same time. Naomi had been widowed some years earlier. Now Naomi, Ruth, and Orpah were all widows. In those times a widow had an extremely difficult life; poverty and loneliness faced such women.

After the deaths of her sons, Naomi decided to return to her home of Bethlehem. However, she released her daughters-in-law from any obligation and encouraged them to return to their own homes and to marry again. Orpah accepted the offer; however, Ruth refused to leave her mother-in-law:

> I will go wherever you go and live wherever you live. Your people will be my people, and your God will be my God. I will die where you die and will be buried there. May the Lord punish me severely if I allow anything but death to separate us. (Ruth 1:16-17, NLT)

Ruth's sense of kindness and compassion continued when they arrived in Bethlehem.

One day Ruth said to Naomi, "Let me go out into the fields to gather leftover grain behind anyone who will let me do it." And Naomi said, "All right, my daughter, go ahead." So Ruth went out to gather grain behind the harvesters. And, as it happened, she found herself working in a field that belonged to Boaz, the relative of her father-in-law, Elimelech." (Ruth 2: 2-3, NLT)

Ruth's act of selflessness and kindness did not go unrewarded. Boaz, a very generous, wealthy, and influential man in Bethlehem, provided her with protection, work, food, and water. Ruth was overwhelmed with such actions on Boaz's part and questioned his behavior:

"Why are you being so kind to me?" she asked. "I am only a foreigner." "Yes, I know," Boaz replied. "But I also know about the love and kindness you have shown your mother-in-law since the death of your husband. I have heard how you left your father and mother and your own land to live here among complete strangers. May the Lord, the God of Israel, under whose wings you have come to take refuge, reward you fully." (Ruth 2:10-12, NLT)

Naomi counseled Ruth, so that Ruth would find further favor with Boaz.

So Boaz took Ruth and she became his wife. . . and bore a son. Then the women said to Naomi, "Blessed be the name of the Lord, who has not left you this day without next-of-kin.". . . Then Naomi took the child and laid him at her bosom and became his nurse. The women of the neighborhood gave him a name saying, "A son has been born to Naomi." They named him Obed; he became the father of Jesse, the father of David. (Ruth 4:13-17)

WHEN WE CHOOSE TO SEE
BEYOND OURSELVES

∞

When we choose to see beyond ourselves, is the beginning of relationship. It is a choice that can move us from isolation, stalemate, and the burdensome feeling that we, and only we, can care for our own destiny. Ruth and Naomi were in a relationship cemented by family and obligation. But it was love and compassion for each other that enriched their ability to see beyond themselves and to contribute more deeply to the lives of each other.

Both Ruth and Naomi were widows in a time and place that sentenced them to poverty and a life of great trial and tribulation. If she were not wealthy, a widow could be taken in by family members, where she would become simply another mouth to feed. If she were young, then she had a chance for remarriage and the opportunity to rebuild her life through having children and contributing to the family. Many widows, though, were abandoned.

Naomi knew her daughters-in-law had only one chance to find a better life, and that would be through marriage. Naomi released both her daughters from their obligation to stay with her. Naomi showed compassion by looking beyond her own uncertain future to seeing the plight of two young women of childbearing age who were without husbands. Ruth, however, looked back at Naomi and saw an old woman who had little chance for a better life—and possibly would not even survive. Nevertheless, Ruth chose to stay with Naomi and help to support her. Perhaps both Naomi and

Ruth recognized what it would be like to be abandoned and left to struggle on her own.

Does this story surprise us? Why would Ruth and Naomi act out of compassion for each other? Does how well you know someone make a difference in being a compassionate person? Why do *we* act with compassion?

Many reasons are given for acting compassionately toward another. They cluster around our moral or religious belief system and our understanding of how we should act toward one another. "We're all in this together, so we should help one another out," "Because, if it were me in that situation, I'd want someone to help or pay attention," "Because I will be a better person for helping another in need," "It makes for a better world," "I am my brother's keeper," "I have a felt kinship with humanity," and "Do unto others as you would have them do unto you," are commonly voiced.

What do we mean by compassion? A common notion of compassion is a sympathetic response to the misfortune of another and the desire to alleviate the suffering. *We view compassion as a measure of how deeply we choose to see beyond ourselves and how deeply we choose to respond to what we see.*

Compassion denotes that we view another in a situation of struggle, but not necessarily crisis. Struggle can be positive, such as when we struggle to learn a new computer program, or when we struggle to adapt to a new work team. There is hope of moving toward a goal or finding a way out of the situation. However, struggle can also be very negative when we feel overwhelmed, despairing and see no way out. We empathize with all types of struggle and suffering others encounter in daily life.

What are we connecting with as we tune in to the struggles and suffering of others? Something catches our attention.

We feel a pull toward something that is partly familiar, yet at the same time uncomfortably strange. We suspend our focus on our wants, needs, and worries and move our attention to that which has drawn us in.

Initially, we perceive a *surface* view of the other. We generally take a surface view of many people we encounter, those who come and go in our daily work and life with whom we will have little or no future contact. We extend to them a general sense of kindness, politeness, respect, and honesty.

We also may take a surface view of those with whom we have no direct contact. We hear an announcement on *CNN News* that a major local company is laying off 3000 employees. We watch a woman in a wheelchair at the mall. We are not in a personal relationship with the woman or the employees, but their *situations* have caught our attention; we reflect on them and feel some level of empathy.

However, when we choose to see beyond ourselves even more deeply, we encounter an individual or situation at a more *intimate* level. When we are in a familiar relationship with a colleague, mentor, friend, or golf buddy, we are privileged to gain access to their personal struggles and we broaden our understanding of the barriers they have to overcome. We have a greater sense of empathy for them because of the depth of the relationship. If the woman at the mall is your mother, best friend, or coworker, then a greater level of empathy and understanding of the barriers she faces will most likely be acknowledged.

We can also choose to see another's situation more deeply because we have had a similar experience. Perhaps you have been laid off from a job or you have been involved in making decisions about who will be laid off. You will be more capable of empathizing deeply with those going through the same struggle and pain.

Compassion is not a solitary experience. It erupts into action toward others. How do we choose to respond to what we have seen beyond ourselves?

Our choice of response can also be thought of in terms of the *depth of response*. We respond by giving of our personal interest and time and of our resources, all of which can be thought about incrementally and with tongue-in-cheek as "a token," "a hit the wallet," and "a major investment."

A "token" represents a lower level of compassionate response, which requires minimal sacrifice of personal interest, time, and/or resources. The intermediate level, "a hit in the wallet," signifies greater sacrifice or effort by an individual or organization. "Major investment" entails extensive interest, time, resources, and risks that are directed toward the struggle of an individual, group, or environment.

A story is told by a retired employee of Ford Motor Company about a colleague and friend who had worked at a General Motors production plant in Mexico. The plant was built in an area where many of the employees were living at poverty level. This plant executive wanted to express a "token" of his appreciation for his workers and also do something that the employees were not able to afford. He took everyone out to lunch at a restaurant chosen by the employees. This same executive was disturbed that many employees had to buy clothing for work that took money away from basic needs in employee's homes. He helped establish a policy stipulating that a work outfit (shirts and pants) be provided by the corporation for the employees.[24] This might be thought of as a "hit in the wallet" level of compassionate response, requiring a significant but not inordinate investment. A "major investment" would be where the corporation invests heavily in education, health benefits, and good working conditions for employees and in the health, safety, and viability of their community life beyond the work environment.

It is interesting that this type of story circulated among auto executives and served to strengthen an appreciation for the social contributions that an executive and his organization could make. We recognize this need within ourselves to contribute to the welfare of others, whether we call it "lending a supportive and friendly hand," "providing great service," or "being socially responsible." We, like the GM executive, engage in all these levels of compassionate response. One is not necessarily better than the other; we respond to the degree we see beyond ourselves and the degree to which we are willing to give.

Dave Thomas, the founder of Wendy's restaurants, has served as a wonderful example of this spirit of compassion.[25] Now in his late sixties, and after a massive heart attack and bypass surgery, Thomas seems to be on a mission.

Since 1989 he has appeared on more than 600 television commercials. You would think, given his age and health history, he would slow down and retire. But he points out that being on TV makes people aware of who he is and that provides him with credibility to reach the people who can make a difference in the lives of the less fortunate. It also provides him with the resources to provide concrete support.

Dave Thomas devotes his time and effort to helping children in need. He has a special empathy for these children, since he himself was adopted as a child and grew up in poverty. Over the years Thomas has donated more than $20 million to help children, and he continues to give. Perhaps even more important, he generously gives of his time. Recognizing that his life would have been even more difficult had he not been adopted, he focuses much of his efforts on trying to help children in need of adoption. He has traveled extensively, meeting with the heads of companies and asking them to provide adoption benefits to their employees, something that Wendy's has provided for years. Wendy's not only provides assistance with the costs of adoption but also offers the same leave benefits that parents of natural children receive.

A striking attribute of Dave Thomas is the extent to which he demonstrates what he advocates in his own life. During his travels, Thomas visits with children in a variety of settings, from foster care to high schools to colleges. His constant message focuses on the value of getting an education. At the age of 60, Thomas received his high-school diploma after studying and passing the General Equivalency Exam. He took his wife of 45 years to the prom and donned a cap and gown for the graduation ceremonies along with nearly 500 other students at Coconut Creek High School in Florida. The other graduates voted him Most Likely to Succeed!

Dave Thomas, Ruth, and Naomi have chosen to see beyond themselves, and their compassionate actions serve as a beacon for us. Their stories have prompted us to consider the importance of a point of entry into the lives of others. Something caught their attention, they identified with what they saw, and they responded deeply of themselves. This leads us to ask, how do *we* choose to see beyond ourselves and what is our response?

WHEN WE WALK
IN A FOREIGN LAND

∞

My husband and I stopped at a small plumbing supply shop one rainy Thursday afternoon. No one was in the store except the owner-manager, who was on the phone. He was working at a desk that was buried in the back of the small showroom crammed with tubs, sinks, and toilets, plus an enormous green marble jacuzzi, the centerpiece of the store.

We were considering renovating our master bath and had a small shower space that would need some type of custom base. The lead to this out-of-the-way place came from a regional home and garden show we had attended a month earlier. The manager continued his long-winded sales talk, his conversation sprinkled with "I'll do whatever it takes," and "I guarantee whatever we do." After a 10-minute wait, we had exhausted both our survey of the items on the floor and our patience.

Just then the manager hung up the phone, apologized for the wait, and made his way over to us. He was a young man of medium build, thirty-ish, with stylish glasses. Within a short time, we realized he primarily handled cultured marble bath and kitchen items. After downplaying the quality and market of name-brand solid-surface products, he proceeded into a sales pitch about cultured marble and its value, durability, and manufacturing process. "I can make any size, any shape you want." His style of speech and tone seemed an outdated sales approach; it was not, to me, "consumer friendly."

I was on the verge of walking out of the store after having been talked at for several minutes in this manner. I had already tuned him out and no longer really heard what he was saying. He threw out names of local "wealthy people" in the area for whom he had done work. This evidently was to impress us, but because we were not from that area we had no idea who he was talking about, nor did we care. He was very attuned to his small-town area, where it became evident most of his business was done. As I inched my way toward the centerpiece jacuzzi, and the front door, I heard him say something about a neighborhood of "old, retired people" and "replacing tubs with showers."

What did he say? My attention was snagged in my unconscious and slowly rose to the surface. I had just spent the past year saturated with the worries and concerns of a critically ill parent and issues revolving around either adapting the current home for frail elderly use, or selling the home and moving my parent into an assisted living facility. I was immersed in the issues of occupational therapy, physical therapy, home nursing, and all the parameters of navigating in and out of a house, a bed, and a bath area. I knew how important it was for the elderly to have a safe, usable bathroom and to remain in their own home.

He explained that he had removed the tubs from these small houses where people had lived for years and were now retired. He then replaced the tub with a shower base that would allow wheelchair access. He had done "tons of these." I now listened to every word he said and I brightened up. "You're doing really good work!" I exclaimed. "This is very important!" And I shook his hand in my enthusiasm. We connected in a new way and his whole manner changed.

He relaxed and answered my questions. He continued to point out things we needed to consider in renovating our bathroom, even after sensing that we might not be customers of his after all.

All of our spirits had been lifted. We thanked him and my husband I moved beyond the centerpiece jacuzzi, through the front door, and into the rainy drizzle of a Thursday afternoon.

When we go to a foreign land, we feel the shock of contrast at the differences in language, dress, food, architecture, and, perhaps especially, at the different way of doing things. These are obvious differences, the kinds that Ruth had to encounter when she moved to Bethlehem with Naomi. But on a day-to-day basis, we don't have to travel far to encounter our own cultural versions of the differences that can exist between teenager and adult, worker and manager, male and female, urban and rural, and even between salesperson and customer. These differences may be obvious or may be subtle, as in the case of the plumbing supply shop.

How do we navigate and negotiate these differences? A compassionate stance and open communication are a solid beginning. Good communication, especially between very different individuals or groups, and compassion build upon the same base. In our chapter on Ruth, we introduce a view of compassion as being how deeply we choose to see beyond ourselves and how deeply we choose to respond to what we see. We "see" the other person, we identify with that situation at either a surface or deeper level, and then we respond. Our ability to extend ourselves to the other person or situation and be open to a common connection is crucial for relationship building and workplace effort. It can make or break sales interactions, contract negotiations, employee trust and morale, and efficient performance that is dependent upon good communication

Cross-cultural communication is dependent upon a respect for the other culture and on individuals from each culture who can serve as trusted guides. This allows us to mediate differences in our search for common places to connect. Naomi served as Ruth's trusted and faithful guide through a strange land. Naomi guided Ruth in relating with people, especially Boaz, and also in getting work in the barley fields that provided for their livelihood. Ruth respected and trusted Naomi, which allowed Ruth to be successful in making important, life-sustaining connections with her new land.

Subtle differences in communication expectations and patterns can create wide gulfs between individuals, especially those we think we know well. In the plumbing-supply scenario, different styles of communication are operating as well as different expectations about "how things are done" between salesperson and customer. The salesperson was focused on the product and pigeonholed me as his stereotypical customer. He spoke *at* me, with mostly useless information. I, however, was hopeful for some trustworthy connection with him whereby a two-way dialogue could develop based on his sense of *me*, not a stereotype. In some respects, I did feel as if I were standing in a foreign land.

I tuned the manager out after failed attempts to find that connection. However, when I heard something with which I could connect in a more meaningful way, I was drawn back into the conversation and able to establish a different rapport with him. Our work was completed, from my perspective, when I obtained the information I sought, and we left in better relationship than when we first met. But, you may ask, did the salesperson complete *his* work, did he make a sale? No, he did not make a sale, but he provided fertile ground for helping us all reflect on the task of work that goes beyond performance to include open communication and trustworthy relationships with others.

Ruth and Naomi point to the necessity for relying on respect and trusting communication for worklife relationships and life security. Naomi was intent on finding a husband for Ruth, which would ensure Ruth's livelihood. Naomi was also instrumental in helping Ruth to glean the fields to provide temporarily for their daily subsistence. Ruth was successful in finding a husband, Boaz, who would end up providing for both Ruth and Naomi's security.

Ruth would become the mother of a son, Obed. Naomi became the child's nursemaid. Obed later fathered Jesse, who fathered King David. And of course, David was the father of King Solomon. This lineage led to a time of great wisdom and prosperity. Over time, our own interactions can lead to greater wisdom and prosperity if we take daily steps to open ourselves to others and allow ourselves to walk in foreign lands with faith and compassion.

WHEN WE SEE AND VALUE
OTHERS AS OURSELVES

∞

Two of the most potent and seemingly contradictory business concepts are competition and cooperation. Competition is a revered concept in our society; it is sometimes considered synonymous with excellence. We have certainly received benefits from the motivation and incentive that competition can stimulate. In a capitalistic society, competition can encourage innovation, improved efficiency, better service, and a host of other potentially positive outcomes. Unfortunately, competition can also become destructive. Sometimes people are moved to place much greater value on short-term performance and winning than on the individuals involved. Ethics, morals, and a positive sense of what's right can take a back seat to the pursuit of victory. Short-term performance is given priority over relationships. With competition, all too often personal gain comes to overshadow everything else.

The story of Ruth offers us some important insights about the trade-off between personal gain and serving others; it pulls cooperation into the equation. This in turn may help put competition in a new light. When Ruth's husband died, she was at high risk of becoming destitute. With Ruth's sister-in-law recently widowed and their widowed mother-in-law, Naomi, it was clear that this three-woman household was in dire straights. Ruth's best chance for a better life was to remarry. Naomi encouraged Ruth to return to her people and do just that, but Ruth would have none of it. She had developed a positive relationship with Naomi. She realized her mother-in-law was likely too old to remarry and would be in a near-ly hopeless situation if left on her own. She felt a compassion and loyalty for her mother-in-law that transcended her own personal gain.

Ruth's choice can hit many of us right where we live. Our lives repeatedly tend to encounter situations where hard choices must be made. Events often raise the question "Will we respond to our desire to gain what we want for ourselves or will we reflect more deeply on what is best for others involved?" "Will we ruthlessly compete or cooperate for mutual benefit?" "Will we focus on how we relate to others, or on short-term performance and personal gain?" Consider a dramatic example of this challenge that was encountered by an individual, appropriately, in the competitive context of a race.

Jon Bowen was running a 10K (6.2 miles) race, the Harvest Moon Classic in Washington, D.C. He had trained very hard for the race and was on target for a personal best time as he neared the half-way point. Suddenly, the runner in front of him twisted his ankle in a pothole and fell to the cement. Mr. Bowen described what happened this way:

> To capture a 40-minute personal record, all I had to do was hold my pace during these last miles. Then the guy in front of me went down. He rolled onto his back and clutched his ankle with his hands. In one fleeting moment, the time it takes to cover 5 meters at a near sprint, I had to decide whether to stop or sail on past. Right there, I ran smack up against morality's old dichotomy: duty to fellow man or every man for himself.

Bowen had come face to face with Ruth's choice. He continued his account:

I didn't stop to help the guy. In fact, I hurdled over him so I wouldn't lose precious seconds by going around him. A little further on, I glanced back over my shoulder and saw that another racer, a woman, had stopped to help the guy to his feet. I finished the race, and I got my PR [personal record], but it bothered me then—and it still does—that in one of life's little definitive moments, I made the selfish choice.

The novelist Ian McEwan says "Selfishness is written in our hearts." Compassion is written there too. The dilemma, when you're pushing toward the finish line, is knowing when to let compassion take the lead. Next time, I hope to make the right choice." [26]

A story like this can call us to rethink what is important in competition. To borrow from the lines in a popular movie, "Sometimes when you win you lose. . . and sometimes when you lose you win."[27] Clearly Joe Bowen regretted his choice in not helping another. He did win, in the sense that he ran the race in a personal best time, but he lost in a deeper sense. He made a choice of performance over compassion and relationship that haunted him at a deeper moral and perhaps spiritual level.

It seems that Ruth understood this, as did the runner who stopped to help in the above story. They both seemed to know that if they made the choice that would provide them with the greatest potential personal gain, the clearest path to winning personally, then they would lose in a way that would never compensate for what they had gained.

In a sense, Ruth had been invited to simply run past her fallen traveling companion, her mother-in-law. Naomi told Ruth that she had been very good to her and had done all that

Naomi could ever have expected of her. She released Ruth from any further duty to her, but Ruth did not hesitate to delay her life journey and try to help. Ruth beseeched Naomi to let her stay. Perhaps Ruth recognized that the freedom would carry with it an even greater burden.

In the business world, examples of hard choices that would seem to fly in the face of a competitive perspective are made more often than we might think. For example, a multitude of companies have adopted a cooperative stance by relying on empowered teams in their work structures. Much of the impetus for this approach is what is generally called a socio-technical perspective. As the label implies, this perspective calls for a balanced emphasis on the social (relationship) and the technical (performance) aspects of organizations. The philosophy calls for a view that combines an emphasis on relationships between people and performance of the work.

Workers are often rotated in job positions so that they can better understand the challenges and difficulties that others on their team face when they perform a task. Many companies pay their employees based on the number of jobs they learn and encourage them to learn many jobs across multiple teams. The resulting spirit of empathy and understanding can promote a more cooperative and compassionate environment, where individuals try to help one another succeed rather than just "looking out for Number One."

Within these work systems, employees are assigned social and task responsibilities and evaluated based on the quality of their social relationships as well as their task performance. The often-perceived choice between performance and relationship is removed; both are part of the job.

AES corporation, an independent energy-producing

company, encourages an intense team spirit throughout the entire company. AES de-emphasizes profit as a primary motive in favor of a set of what sound like noncompetitive values, including integrity, fairness, fun, and social responsibility. They list the names of every employee in the company in the annual report—a list that spanned some thirty-five pages of a recent report. They also adopted a tradition of sending their top executives out to various AES sites, where they roll up their sleeves and go to work on tasks the local employees assign them. This practice keeps them connected with their workforce and promotes an understanding of the challenges company employees face. AES has excelled with its apparent noncompetitive competitiveness; with their cooperative spirit, they have made *Fortune*'s list of America's fastest-growing companies.

Organizations are discovering more and more that successfully competing in their industries requires effective cooperation. Relationship and performance does go hand-in-hand. A focus on serving rather than trying to achieve personal gain through manipulation, intimidation, or other tactics can promote higher performance as well as a more supportive and compassionate workplace. Not only does cooperation create a more positive environment in which to work but it also fosters an ethical spirit of treating others fairly.

Sometimes wisdom leads us to unexpected places, and the lessons we can glean about competition provide a good case in point. Very often cooperation with a spirit of service can supplant competition as the best way to achieve prosperity (financial health, social benefit, and peace of mind) even within seemingly highly competitive situations.

ARE WE THEN CALLED TO
BETTER SERVE?

∾

We have been looking at some of the issues surrounding the tension between the need to perform the tasks of our work and the need and desire to be in relationship with people as we accomplish our work. Let us consider a few questions to guide our continuing search for wisdom in our workplaces.

Task vs. Relationship

"You know James, this job of yours. . . it's murder on relationships."

Mrs. Paris Carver to James Bond,
in the movie *Tomorrow Never Dies*

Can you think of a time when you decided to not play the game of competition, focusing instead on helping or supporting another? What was the outcome? How did you feel about it? In what ways is your work related to concern for people?

Communication

Newspaper Ad: Back Bay Shutter Co.
"100% Service / 0% Attitude"

What message is this ad trying to convey? What attitudes do you think are important for providing good service? How does your attitude about service affect your ability to communicate?

Wisdom Incorporated

Dear Ann, [28]

I've been a registered nurse for 32 years. The bean counters have made it impossible for patients to receive good care. We are understaffed and over-worked, and we grit our teeth trying to provide the quality care our patients deserve. I'm exhausted, disillusioned and heartsick. (NYC)

Don't blame the hospitals for overworked nurses. The insurance companies and HMOs have too much control over healthcare, and they are calling the shots. It's all about the bottom line, Money! Money! Money!" (Columbia, MO)

I'm a Brit who worked in three hospitals in England. I loved it. When I came to the United States, I passed my boards easily but found nursing so depressing, I had to get out. I discovered it was a business, not a calling. (Alta Loma, California)

What is the issue here? What do you think are some of the constraints these nurses are facing in their work situations? Can a compassionate stance be used to help address the *business as usual* values imbedded in these employee frustrations? How?

Service

"Superior service is more than enabling technology and intelligent service system design, although both are exceedingly important. Superior serving also is human artistry and attitude and spontaneous decision-making and physical effort and mental energy. It is skills and knowledge and judgment. It is commitment, caring, and confidence."[29]

How do *you* define service? Where are you called to provide service? How do you answer the call?

The Integrity and
Justice of Moses

THE STORY OF MOSES

(Adapted from the Books of Exodus and Deuteronomy)

∞

Moses was the first great leader of the Hebrews, and to him is attributed authorship of the first five books of the Old Testament. These books, Genesis through Deuteronomy, are known as the Torah in the Hebrew Bible. Moses was born in Egypt when the Hebrews were enslaved to Pharaoh, the ruler of Egypt. Moses' mother hid her baby until Moses was three months old because she didn't want him to be killed by the Egyptians:

> When she could hide him no longer she got a papyrus basket for him, and plastered it with bitumen and pitch; she put the child in it and placed it among the reeds on the bank of the river. (Exodus 2:3)

The basket with Moses inside was discovered by the Pharaoh's daughter. Upon seeing this, Moses' sister asked the Pharaoh's daughter, "Shall I go and get you a nurse from the Hebrew women to nurse the child for you?" The Pharaoh's daughter said yes. Moses' sister brought back a Hebrew woman, Moses' own mother. Pharaoh's daughter remarked to Moses' mother, "Take this child and nurse it for me, and I will give you your wages." So she took her own child and was paid to nurse him. (Exodus 2:7-9)

Later when Moses was old enough, his mother took him back to the Pharaoh's daughter, who adopted him as her own son. Moses was then raised in a royal home and enjoyed luxurious surroundings and received a superior education.

As Moses grew up in the house of Pharaoh, he became a very wise and distinguished man. Moses knew that he was not Egyptian and that his parents were Israelite slaves. One day, Moses decided to visit his people, the Hebrews, and what he found was unsettling to him. He witnessed an Egyptian beating a Hebrew. Moses decided to act. When he thought no one was watching, Moses hit the Egyptian, killing him, and buried the corpse in the sand.

The next day, Moses went among his people with the intention of helping to free them from slavery. He saw two Israelite men fighting and responded to the one in the wrong: "Why do you strike your fellow Hebrew?" The man answered, "Who made you ruler and judge over us? Do you mean to kill me as you killed the Egyptian?" (Exodus 2:13, 14). The Hebrews viewed Moses' killing as an arrogant use of his power.

When Pharaoh heard about the Egyptian's death, he sent men to kill Moses. Moses then fled Egypt for the country of Midian. In Midian, Moses married Zipporah, daughter of Jethro. Moses became a shepherd and took care of his father-in-law's sheep for many years.

After a long time, the Pharaoh died, and a cry to God went up from the Israelites that they be released from slavery. God responded by calling on Moses from within a burning bush that was not consumed by the fire. He told Moses that He had seen and heard the suffering of the Hebrews in Egypt and that He wanted Moses to lead the Hebrews out of Egyptian slavery.

Moses responded, "Who am I that I should go to Pharaoh, and bring the Israelites out of Egypt?" (Exodus 3:11). God instructed Moses to tell the Israelites that God himself had sent him to free the Israelites. Moses questioned

God: "But suppose they do not believe me or listen to me, but say 'The Lord did not appear to you?'" (Exodus 4:1). To convince the Israelites, Moses was told by God to show them several miracles. These included turning a stick into a snake, making Moses' hand the color of snow, and turning water into blood.

Though the Israelites saw Moses perform these miracles, the Pharaoh was not impressed. The Pharaoh worked the slaves harder than ever. Moses became frustrated and discouraged with his efforts to free his people and complained to God but God told Moses to remain faithful. He would not abandon the people of Israel. God responded by bringing ten plagues on Egypt. Finally, after enduring the tenth plague, of death to every Egyptian firstborn child and animal, Pharaoh released the Israelites from captivity (Exodus 7-11).

However, soon thereafter, the Pharaoh had a change of heart and decided to try to recapture the Israelites. With his army, he began to pursue Moses and his people. Moses, with the support of God, helped the Israelites overcome obstacles to their escape, including parting the Red Sea so that the Israelites could march through it.

> As Pharaoh drew near, the Israelites looked back, and there were the Egyptians advancing on them. . . But Moses said to the people, "Do not be afraid, stand firm". . . . Then Moses stretched out his hand over the sea. The Lord drove the sea back by a strong east wind all night, and turned the sea into dry land; and the waters were divided. (Exodus 14:10-21)

When the Egyptian army tried to pursue the Israelites into the Red Sea, the waters closed upon them and they were drowned. Afterward, the Israelites wandered in the desert for 40 years. Through their God they received the rituals and laws, including the Ten Commandments, that governed their daily life.

This was a harsh time for the Israelites; the people became tired and felt lost. Moses had to deal continually with complaints from his people. His people were discouraged and, on occasion, Moses was discouraged. But with God's help, Moses was able to maintain his faithfulness.

Ultimately, Moses succeeded in delivering the Israelites to their promised land.

> And the Lord showed him [Moses] the whole land: Gilead as far as Dan, all Naphtali, the land of Ephraim and Manessah, all the land of Judah as far as the Western Sea, the Negeb, and the Plain—that is, the valley of Jerico, the city of palm trees—as far as Zoar. The Lord said to him, "I will give it to your descendants; I have let you see it with your own eyes, but you shall not cross over there." Then Moses, the servant of the Lord, died in the land of Moab, at the Lord's command. Moses was 120 years old when he died; his sight was unimpaired and his vigor had not abated. (Deuteronomy 34:1-7)
>
> Never since has there arisen a prophet in Israel like Moses, whom the Lord knew face to face. He was unequaled for all the signs and wonders that the Lord sent him to perform in the land of Egypt, against Pharaoh and all his servants and his entire land, and for all the mighty deeds and all the terrifying displays of power that Moses performed in the sight of all Israel. (Deuteronomy 34:10-12)

WHEN WE ARE CALLED TO LEAD
AND FEEL INADEQUATE

∞

God said to Moses, "Go, I will send you to Pharaoh and demand that he let you lead my people out of Egypt." "Who me?" exclaimed Moses. "I'm not the person for a job like that!"

A call to leadership is one of the greatest challenges we can face. Consider the word *leader* and what it means. For many, a leader means someone superior and special. The implication is that we should be able to do all and know all. Of course, this mental baggage is too heavy for most of us to carry. That is, we face a resistance to lead in ways similar to Moses. Why is this?

To get at this question, we can first ask "What was Moses' idea of being a leader and why did he balk at it?" He countered God's call by pointing out he was not a good speaker and that he had a speech impediment. Surely the people would not listen to him. Perhaps more important, Moses feared that his weakness would be exposed. But God offered a solution: he would let Moses' brother Aaron speak with Moses' guidance. Thus, even though Moses lacked the communication skill that he believed a leader must have, God still called him to lead and in the process sent a message that leadership is more than just oratory skill.

Yet one is left wondering whether Moses felt more inadequate when meeting God face to face or when God assigned him to be leader of the Israelites. Such is the magnitude of the challenge of leading. Moses was indeed a man of integrity, but did he feel that he had the knowledge, the skills, and the strength of character to undertake such a leadership challenge? Clearly he found himself lacking; this was perhaps his greatest qualification in God's eyes. God wanted someone who was faithful, rather than a self-made warrior.

God chose Moses to lead because of his virtues: he was faithful, compassionate, and just, a man of integrity. The leadership knowledge and skills would follow if Moses would work with God and his people to deliver them to the promised land. In many ways, for Moses and the rest of us, leadership calls us to journey on an inner path. We have to face our inner struggles before we are adequately equipped to take on the challenge of leading in the external world.

Moses agreed to answer the call and he went to Egypt, but his struggles with reconciling his human imperfection with the challenge of being a leader were only beginning.

Often the burden of leadership is simply too great for one person to carry. Moses had to learn to work with others to get the job done. He adjusted to being a leader who relied on someone else to be his voice. Later, when Moses found himself listening to the complaints of the Israelites from morning to evening, his father-in-law Jethro challenged him directly. He asked Moses why he tried to serve as the sole judge for the disagreements of the people. He pointed out that he was taking far too much time and that the people had to stand around all day long waiting for Moses to hear their problems. He asked why Moses was doing this work all by himself.

When Moses tried to defend his single-handed leadership Jethro responded that it was not right and that he would soon wear himself out, leaving the people without a leader. He instructed Moses to find capable and honest men who would not be tempted by bribes to serve as judges, one judge for every thousand people. He suggested that each of these judges have ten judges under them that would each be responsible for one hundred people. And under them would be two judges, each responsible for fifty people; these judges would have five judges under them who would counsel ten persons.

Anything too complicated for the judges to handle would be brought to Moses, but less difficult matters would be handled by the other judges. Jethro pointed out that this would lighten Moses' load because he would be sharing the burden, and it would enable him to endure the many pressures he faced as leader.* In essence, Jethro taught Moses that good leadership involves and empowers others to help with the process, that a good leader does not try to shoulder the entire burden of justice alone.

Moses faced other serious leadership struggles. One of his greatest fears was that his people and Pharaoh would ignore him. In response, God provided Moses with the ability to accomplish great miracles; he turns the water in the river to blood, parts the Red Sea, and causes great plagues, so that his leadership would be taken seriously.

"What do I do?" Moses repeatedly asked of God. Many times, God directly responded with guidance. Other times, Moses acted based on his understanding of God's purposes and according to his faith tradition and the scriptures. Throughout his difficult leadership journey, he leaned on God as his guide and source of strength.

---

*Some credit Moses with creating the first bureaucracy when he established this system of justice, but he delegated power and authority in ways not usually identified with bureaucracies.

Leaders are often criticized or ignored, and Moses was no exception. This negative reaction can occur when leaders are doing what they sincerely believe is right. Perhaps the sting is even more painful because they care about others and are trying so hard to do what they believe will benefit everyone. In such times it can be very difficult to stay the course. Moses personified important spiritual virtues, but this did not make his life easier. He continually faced challenges and struggles, along with the cries and complaints of his people. The faithful leader suffered in both the best and worst of times.

Former President Jimmy Carter, like Moses, has been widely criticized as a leader, and many questioned the strength of his leadership.[30] Most notably, he was rejected by his people for a second term in office. Despite significant presidential accomplishments that many did not recognize, Carter seems to have bloomed in his post-presidential role. In fact, he has arguably been the most successful former American President. In all of this, Carter has clearly lived a life as a spiritually grounded person.

As a former president, Carter has been very active internationally in helping to resolve conflicts. He worked to resolve the nuclear stalemate with North Korea, to achieve a cease-fire in Sudan, to achieve a peaceful occupation of Haiti, and to establish a cease-fire in Bosnia. He created the Carter Center at Emory University to provide a place where people can come together to resolve conflicts. Indeed, Carter seems to have had the most remarkable influence after he left the Oval Office.

Even more striking evidence that he is a spiritually grounded person has been Carter's work for Habitat for Humanity, a non-profit organization that helps provide housing for the poor and the homeless. Carter is a striking model as he rolls up his sleeves and grabs a hammer or saw and goes to work. He provides a persuasive example of a flawed yet remarkable human being who cares enough about his people to provide important leadership in the choices he makes and the way he lives.

Carter has experienced a great deal of criticism and complaining from others. His leadership was repeatedly brought into question and many did not take him seriously. But over his life journey he has stayed the course, remaining faithful to his spiritual beliefs. Perhaps his greatest leadership contribution, like Moses, is contained in the way he has lived; he has modeled a way for his people to be.

The legacy of leadership left by Moses is at once surprising and compelling. He was a leader who declared himself unfit to lead. Nevertheless, he accepted the challenge of God's call. Even as he carried the gauntlet of leadership he seemed continually to stumble over the boulder of his own unrealistic views of leadership. He tried to shoulder the entire load, to be a solitary judge and the sole deliverer of God's word. But he found himself overburdened. He relied on sources of strength beyond himself. His story is of a person who appeared to be sorely inadequate, yet Moses became a great historical leader

In the end, his leadership took on a transcendent quality. He was not a great orator, nor was he an adequate judge for all his people. But the way he lived demonstrated implicit principles for living a faithful life. He delivered God's laws and rules to his people, including the bedrock guidelines provided in the Ten Commandments and he delivered his people to the promised land.

Nevertheless, Moses likely made his greatest contribution as a leader in a way that he himself failed to recognize. He was an honest man who earnestly tried to live faithful to the highest calling of his people. He served as a living example of the true path to the promised land, one that lies more within each of us than in some physical place. Moses accomplished what he was challenged by God to do.

WHEN WE SEE THE DARK PITFALLS THAT TRAP OUR PEOPLE

∞

Life is filled with dark holes. Some can be avoided and others we manage to jump. Unfortunately, still others seem to be unavoidable and all too often we fall in. This was true for Moses and his people, as it is for each of us.

Tradition, socialization, insecurity, and a lack of trust all combined to create formidable inner struggles that can lead to dysfunctional action. The Israelites demonstrated wavering faith, and they questioned God and Moses' leadership. They frequently went astray, worshipping false idols and falling into destructive, hedonistic behavior. Ultimately, it became apparent that the greatest pitfalls were in Moses' people.

Moses himself faced many pitfalls stemming from the hardships of his people and the journey. He complained that his people and Pharaoh would not listen to him. He anguished over the complaints of the people about the lack of food and water. He became disheartened at the trials and difficulties they all had to face.

He pleaded with God not to abandon him and to show him the way to lead. He struggled with his own confidence and faith. His limited view of his own ability to lead became a pitfall. He was inhibited from connecting with and empowering his people in the way they needed.

In the end Moses persevered and he helped his people to do the same, but this is not always the way leadership stories unfold. Sometimes leaders fail in significant ways as they face challenges and hardships.

Part of the problem lies in the way we view leadership. An unfortunate assumption about leadership is that it must involve the external influence (even control and manipulation) of others we call "followers." This is especially troubling when we consider that nearly always each person has the greatest insight into his or her own situation, needs, and motivations. While urgent circumstances sometimes seem to cry out for strong and inspiring leaders, in a very real sense the separation of leader and follower establishes the root of misguided leadership and a lack of integrity.

A presumption is made that a person authorized to lead can better decide and judge what is right or wrong, worthwhile or worthless. However, this implies that a leader leads in isolation and that followers must be relieved of the burden of being truly responsible for themselves.

We assert that the leader's strength flows from his or her ability to facilitate the self-directed contributions of followers. When followers are empowered the potential for integrity as well as effectiveness is released. Through empowerment followers can gain the potential to pull out of the dark holes that exist within themselves.

Leaders can create a context in which followers become more whole and responsible for themselves. Unfortunately, leadership often moves followers to do just as they are directed and to not think, to not be whole, to not be responsible. This precludes integrity. *Integrity* involves honest attempts to adhere to moral and ethical principles. It can also be defined as the state of being whole, entire, or undiminished. A whole person possesses the power and discretion to make choices and thereby takes responsibility.

Without responsibility, integrity is not possible. We must own a burden or problem before we really connect with it. When a leader acts in a way that separates followers from their pitfalls, the potential for true integrity is squelched. History is replete with stories of soldiers and workers performing destructive, even horrible, acts because they viewed the moral burden as resting on the leader—because they did not take responsibility for their own actions.

Only leadership that truly empowers others to be responsible for and address their own inner struggles is leadership with integrity. When leaders "take charge," they may be blocking the most effective and desirable form of leadership—self-leadership. Self-leadership is the influence, direction, and motivation we provide for ourselves. It is not enough just to influence others toward what seem to be desirable ends, but we must avoid blocking the self-leadership of others, which might lead to even more desirable ends.

Yet this burden brings with it an encouraging promise to help overcome some of the intimidation inherent in being a leader. The designation of leader is a daunting challenge. Leaders are frequently expected to be pillars of strength who have all the answers and solve all the problems.

When leaders believe they must carry the whole load themselves it is not surprising that they often come to feel inadequate, that they are just not up to the challenge. Certainly Moses displayed this kind of hesitancy about his own ability to be a leader. Part of the problem is that when we assume we have to carry the whole burden ourselves, to be our own island as a flawlessly self-sufficient leader, we are in fact inadequate. Moses learned that he needed to rely on God for strength and guidance and that he needed help from his people to meet the seemingly endless challenges of leadership. The next section will look at how Moses learned to shift to others much of the overwhelming burden of serving as sole judge for his peoples' disputes.

One limited person is not enough. Rather, we need everyone to be involved in the process of leadership, we need our followers to be leaders in their own right. That is why the notion of self-leadership provides new hope and a unique source of strength. By viewing leadership as a process of leading others to lead themselves, leaders are freed to enjoy a fresh new role. Elsewhere, this kind of leadership has been referred to as *SuperLeadership* because the leader gains access to the strength of many by unleashing their unique knowledge, experience, creativity, justice, and self-leadership. [31]

Ricardo Semler, the CEO of the very successful Brazilian equipment manufacturer Semco, learned this lesson the hard way.[32] At first he fell prey to leadership myths that push leaders to control and do everything themselves solely for the sake of business outcomes. People became secondary pawns, simply used to obtain bottom-line results. Semler began with a hard-driving disciplinarian style and 18-hour workdays. He tried to carry too much weight on his own shoulders and left too little for employees to feel good about in their own work experience, and all of them suffered. His own health began to fail as he experienced extreme levels of stress and fatigue. Meanwhile his controlling leadership style was creating an apathetic workforce that didn't care, that found little joy in their work, and that produced unsatisfactory performance.

Semler received a strong wake-up call, and he really woke up. He didn't just mouth the words of empowering leadership, he demonstrated it in his own behavior. He cut back on his work hours and shifted his leadership style to an emphasis on empowerment. He created a dynamic environment of self-leadership that radiated a new-found level of integrity and justice. He eliminated nine layers of management and turned over most of the power to his employees. Employees were finally freed to have a significant say in all aspects of the organization and Semler was freed to regain his health and his perspective on what's really important. Some of the characteristics at Semco under Semler's newly empowering leadership included: employees setting their own work hours; the absence of dress codes; employees determining their own salaries; employees sharing over 20 percent of the company's profits; and employees voting on all major company decisions.

In addition, to the unusual level of empowerment and self-leadership afforded Semco's employees under the new system, Semler introduced a number of features that directly contributed to maintaining ongoing integrity while conducting business such as opening the company's financial books to anyone, including all employees. Employees are offered courses on how to read financial statements to make sure they can understand them. Also employees approve the hiring and promotion of their own managers, evaluate their managers twice a year, and regularly evaluate the credibility of the company and top management.

Semco employees truly became responsible, which led to an atmosphere of trust and integrity. Semler described the new atmosphere in very frank business terms: "Employees can paint the walls any color they like. They can work whenever they decide. They can wear whatever clothing makes them comfortable. They can do whatever the hell they want. It's up to them to see the connection between productivity and profit and to act on it." [33]

As a result of Semler's new, enlightened view of leadership, Semco thrived. Productivity shot up 700 percent. Profit increased by 500 percent. Sales increased fivefold. Turnover became almost nonexistent, and a long waiting list of job applicants soon formed. As one employee explained, Semco "became a paradise to work in. Nobody wants to leave." [34]

Of course, a concern may arise here that employees might abuse their new-found power and become self-serving at the expense of others and even themselves. Even in the wake of living much like slaves during their captivity in Egypt, the Israelites abused some of their new freedom when Moses led them toward their promised land. As they journeyed through the desert, they sometimes chose behavior (for example, worshipping idols) that was self-destructive and contradicted their deeply held religious beliefs. Eventually Moses' leadership helped them find their way back to the more virtuous way of living they had originally espoused. But, in the short run, being freed from their slavery simply led them from one problematic situation to another, from one set of pitfalls and dark holes to another.

In organizational settings, empowerment has not been without its problems either. Our own experience has been that when empowerment is first introduced most work systems get worse for a year or two before they get better. Workers need time to adapt and to meet their new challenges (one might argue that the Israelites suffered a similar adjustment process). Many empowerment change efforts are ultimately declared failures. Despite these problems, when real empowerment is put into place with commitment, resources, and training, many companies have enjoyed positive results.

Companies experiencing these benefits firsthand include Fortune 500 power houses such as GM, Ford, Chrysler, GE, Motorola, American Express, Procter & Gamble, Honeywell, Digital Equipment, Boeing, AT&T, Texas Instruments, LTV

Steel, Tektronix, Cummins Engine, among many others. Like Semco, all of these organizations have introduced empowerment somewhere in their organization and experienced a variety of payoffs, ranging from increased productivity, to improved quality, to reduced absenteeism and turnover, to increased innovation and creativity.

An important lesson such pioneering companies have learned is that most employees are fair when they are treated fairly and given a chance to lead themselves. Often the best kind of leadership, modeled so effectively by Ricardo Semler, simply equips so-called followers to do their work well and empowers them to be leaders in their own right. This leadership gets out of the way and allows employees effectively to serve themselves, their fellow workers, the rest of the organization, and the world at large.

Taking on the burden of leading in the face of countless pitfalls calls for a creative new perspective. In a sense, we are challenged to turn leadership upside down, to transform it into something distinctly different. By turning "followers" into their own leaders, we move the whole process to a new place. Followers themselves become a critical source of illumination for seeing and avoiding the dark holes that can entrap them. They learn to lead themselves over and around the pitfalls. Ultimately, many of these potential threats are washed away by the integrity, based on personal responsibility, that is built into the very fabric of leadership as leaders and followers become one and the same.

WHEN WE MUST STAND UP FOR
ALL THE OTHERS

∞

Moses was a leader who faced many personal struggles. He wrestled with doubts, fears, temptations, and frustrations. He sometimes made poor choices but he was a faithful man. In the end this was a central pillar of his leadership. One remarkable quality of Moses was his ability to stand up for others, putting them ahead of himself. Moses repeatedly put himself on the line for his people. He faced Pharaoh and countless other enemies of the Jews, and he even pleaded with God for their welfare. It can be challenging to find leaders who display consistently admirable personal conduct, but leaders who look beyond themselves and stand up for others are rare indeed. In the end, this is perhaps the most striking feature of the intersection of leadership and justice.

Moses was honest and direct with his people and frequently displayed humane leadership that rose above his own needs and welfare to seek their rights. On a number of occasions, Moses intervened for his people when they had gone astray, preventing God from doling out harsh punishment. When Moses ascended Mount Sinai to meet with God, the people soon became restless, assuming that Moses would not return. They molded a golden calf to worship. They offered burnt offerings and engaged in immoral behavior. When God reacted with anger and planned to destroy them, Moses pleaded with God, asking him "to turn back from your (his) fierce wrath," and God spared them.

Of particular historical significance, Moses delivered from

God to his people the Ten Commandments and ritual laws that provided a basis for justice. *Justice* involves the pursuit of moral rightness, fairness, equality, and respect for individual and collective rights. Moses became the vehicle through which God provided a basis for justice and established a new covenant with the people of Israel.

The pursuit of justice, however, can become too heavy a burden for a leader to carry alone. After the Israelites had been led from Egypt, Moses found himself listening to the complaints of the people and serving as judge from morning to evening, day after day. Upon the advice of his father-in-law Jethro, Moses learned that he had to seek the help of other capable and honest men to serve as judges so that he would not be totally consumed by the burden of trying to dole out justice alone.

Outstanding leaders who look beyond themselves and act so as to promote meaningful justice for their followers are greatly needed today. In the last section we examined the leadership of Ricardo Semler at Semco. Clearly the success of Ricardo Semler's empowering leadership style deserves careful attention on the grounds of organizational effectiveness alone. However, an equally important issue concerns the fact that designating employees as leaders (self-leaders) introduces an important check on injustice. In essence each person is empowered to protect a personal level of justice.

For example, Semco employees evaluate and provide crucial input in the selection of their own bosses. They also evaluate major company decisions, top management, and the company itself. Consistent with the spirit of democracy in its purest sense, they are centrally involved in shaping the very system to which they are accountable. Meanwhile, opening the financial books to inspection and asking employees to evaluate the credibility of the company and top management encourages a level of integrity not often enjoyed in business organizations.

The potential for abuse of power is rendered largely impotent as substantial checks and balances are introduced between those leading and those being led. Leaders and followers in a very real sense reverse positions at different points in the work and organizational processes.

Of course, Semco is an unusual example of pushing justice into the very lifeblood of how the organization operates on a daily basis. The story of Moses was also largely one of gaining and maintaining justice. First, the Israelites gained freedom from Egypt. Then, during the journey to the promised land, commandments, ritual laws, and a system of justice based on judges were created. Most organizations concerned with ethics and justice add pieces to the organization to help foster or force moral ends, sometimes in contradiction to the organization's normal business activities. Rights and obligations that are hammered out over long negotiations through labor contracts and union agreements provide traditional examples. More recently, the rise of corporate ethics codes and ethics officers are salient examples of this add-on (or perhaps "force on") approach.

Perhaps the most solid foundation for justice, however, is a leadership commitment to look beyond self to the welfare of others. This is the kind of leadership modeled by Moses. If a leader is sincerely committed to serving others honestly and fairly, then many of the power struggles that give rise to the fight for justice simply become unnecessary.

This is not to say that the issue of justice ever goes away entirely. We are not trying to take a Pollyanna stance that lightly brushes aside the importance of mechanisms to promote justice. Decisions have to be made, and often some individuals and groups stand to benefit more than others, and sometimes, parties are clearly harmed by actions when choices must be made. Thus, the creation of some kind of system for the maintenance of justice is needed. The people of Israel had the Ten Commandments and other ritual laws to guide them. They also had Moses and the others to serve as judges to deal with disputes as they arose.

Nevertheless, opting for adversarial procedures in the pursuit of justice often produces unnecessary injustice. When the norm is to use procedures, regulations, and laws to look out for Number One, there is bound to be conflict and losers. On the other hand, justice can frequently be a natural outcome of an attitude of serving one another that is set by servant leaders who are able to look beyond themselves.[35]

Sir John Templeton is an example of such a servant leader. He has enjoyed remarkable success in business finance. As the founder and former leader of the extremely profitable Templeton Mutual Funds, it would be easy to conclude that he is simply one more savvy businessman who knew how to manage the system to turn modest sums of money into billions for his own personal gain. The interesting difference, however, is that this man believes the most important principles in life are spiritual ones. For years he led the directors of the Templeton Growth Fund in prayer to seek guidance in making wise investment decisions. In fact, Templeton has long believed that practicing spirituality will help you to learn and be more effective in managing your money and life.[36]

Templeton believes all of humankind consists of brothers and sisters who need to care about one another. He points out that, from the beginning, his management of the Templeton

Funds focused on looking beyond himself to help others. Instead of pursuing self-serving wealth, Templeton was driven by a desire to serve others. He espouses principles consistent with the Golden Rule. He believes that by focusing on helping others you will benefit yourself even more than if you focus on your own needs. His most famous strategy in the developing stages of his legendary career was to scour the entire world for investment opportunities (before international investing was fashionable) rather than just investing in the United States. This was arguably based on his belief that all of humanity is connected as one large spiritual family. In doing so, Templeton was able to serve his clients with handsome financial returns as well as to raise money that he could share with worthwhile charitable and spiritual causes. Essentially, he became the liaison for investors to the rest of the financial world.

Templeton's philosophy and dedication to service provide powerful examples of an approach that supplants the "fight for justice." His actions are based on a spiritual and moral foundation and are intended to benefit others rather than seeking personal gain at their expense. When ethical service is the basis for organization practice, justice is built into the fabric of doing business.

Much of Templeton's notable approach to life and leadership can be traced to his early years. As a boy growing up in rural Winchester, Tennessee, the heroes Sir John Templeton most admired were religious missionaries. In fact, his original career goal was to become a missionary. As a Rhodes Scholar at Oxford University, however, he concluded that many others had more talent for missionary work than he did. But he also realized he had considerable talent for managing money and that he could help missionaries more by providing them with the financial resources they needed to do their work than by becoming one of them.

Templeton is a Presbyterian, but he does not favor a single religion for his giving. Rather, he sees value in them all. He was particularly troubled by the lack of progress in understanding human spiritual issues, despite the tremendous advances in other areas such as science and technology, over recent decades. He believed that religion was rapidly losing influence because of its lack of progress in other areas and questioned the tendency of religions to look backward rather than valuing progress. At least in part as a reaction to this concern, he endowed the Templeton Prize for Progress in Religion, the largest philanthropic prize in the world. This is only one of many ways that Templeton has supported advances on spiritual issues. The millions of dollars that he has given support activities as wide-ranging as provision of awards for teens who write essays on spiritual life experiences to distribution of spiritually inspiring books, the bulk of which are coordinated through the large and active Templeton Foundation.

Perhaps the best way to sum up the life of Sir John Templeton is to say that he is, as Moses was, first a spiritual man and second a successful businessman. He believes the ultimate answers to what is important in life can be found in the spiritual domain. The secret to success that he espouses and models in his own life are to grow spiritually and look beyond yourself. He has worked proactively to establish justice throughout the world. Ultimately, he seems to argue most strongly that it is only in looking beyond yourself and serving your fellow human beings that you will grow in wisdom and prosper.

Moses was a leader who learned to stand up for his people. He drew strength and guidance from God and sought help from others to shoulder the burden of leadership. Ultimately it was in looking beyond himself that he was able to provide meaningful service and promote justice for his people. Some modern-day leaders, such as Ricardo Semler and Sir John Templeton, seem to have discovered similar lessons. It appears that the best kind of leadership rests on looking beyond oneself, serving others, and ultimately serving and discovering deeper life meaning. Through this process, the very fabric of life and work become interwoven with the strong strands of fairness, justice, and service.

HOW CAN WE DELIVER?

∞

Let us now shift focus toward putting these ideas into practice. We hope to provide you with a way of reflecting on your own living and leading, and on the place of leadership, integrity, and justice in your own life.

In this section, a number of questions will be raised. We suggest that after reading each question you pause and think about your response. Each question is followed by a mini-essay with some of our thoughts on the issue. We hope this material will provide you with another viewpoint that contains some added insights for your own reflection; our personal thoughts on the issue are not necessarily intended to be *the* answers for you.

Leadership

Leadership is an alluring concept that has captured the fascination of people for thousands of years. Often it is viewed as a quality that is pertinent only to a select few (the privileged, the exceptional); however, we would like to suggest a different view that acknowledges the wider importance of leadership for all of us.

Are you a leader?
First, consider that you are your own ultimate leader. Regardless of the leadership influence you experience from others, you ultimately decide how you will respond and what you will choose to do. You are a self-leader. Beyond this self-

influence you likely have specific influence over others (serve as a leader) in multiple situations in relation to your family, your work, and your connections with many others through your various life activities. Thus, you are a leader. You may not have always thought of yourself that way, but you are. So the more important questions address how you will respond and how you will deliver as a leader. To reflect more deeply on these ideas, consider the following questions.

Do you accept the challenge of leadership in your life? Specifically, where are you called to lead and how do you answer the call?

What are some primary areas where you are in a position to influence others? Think about your family and your work. Who are the people that most need your leadership right now? How can you be of service?

Are your views on leadership realistic? Specifically, can you lead with a recognition of your own limitations?

When we answer a call to lead, it is important to do so with a sense of humility. We are all imperfect human beings and our human knowledge and wisdom is limited. This points to the importance of letting others make their own choices when possible and to live their own lives. When we find ourselves in a position of leadership, especially when it comes with official power assigned to a formal position such as boss or department manager, it is tempting to believe that we know what is best for others. We can easily become drunk with the power, prestige, and importance of it all.

One of the most difficult challenges for Moses was accepting the fact that he could serve as a leader without having to provide all the answers and make all the decisions. Ricardo Semler learned this important lesson when his health began to fail and his employees' morale began to suffer. Like Moses and Semler, we need to accept that at its best leadership is a process that turns followers into leaders in their own right. Ironically, recognizing our limitations lessens the burden we must carry and can make our leadership significantly more effective.

Do you share leadership with others? Specifically, how do you lead others to be their own leaders?
Consider this issue more deeply. In what ways do you help others to develop their ability to lead themselves? How do you help them to gain the confidence to do this on an ongoing basis? When decisions need to be made that others are very capable of handling, this provides an opportunity for facilitating self-leadership in yourself and others. By empowering and encouraging others to make more decisions, you enable them to grow as people. At the same time, as you learn to step back and let others shine, you are developing your own self-discipline and leadership ability.

Probably the easiest thing a leader can do is simply give orders to others and then take credit. It is much more challenging to step out of the spotlight and let others be the focus of attention. By doing so, however, you allow your leadership to be leveraged by the growing multiple talents, capabilities, and expertise of others.

Interestingly, leading others to lead themselves is one of the most powerful self-leadership strategies for a leader. Ricardo Semler, along with many other visible leaders, has learned this important lesson and consequently become far more effective.

Integrity

Now that you have considered the general topic of leadership, we move our focus to the issue of integrity. Again, we will ask several questions to facilitate a spirit of reflection about the place of integrity in your life and your leadership.

Can you see the pitfalls of your followers? Can you see your own pitfalls?

True integrity is founded on a humble recognition of weaknesses and our need for help. Integrity is not a facade. We are human beings with frailties and weaknesses. As leaders, we need to recognize our need for the input and participation of others. We do not have all the answers nor can we make all the decisions. At the same time, we need to recognize the pitfalls of those we lead and try to help them. Often this simply involves helping others to help themselves. Ricardo Semler provided leadership in this spirit at Semco, and Jimmy Carter has adopted this spirit in his post-presidency leadership.

What does integrity mean to you? Do you model integrity?

Actions do speak louder than words. Moses continually had to back up his convictions with action and become a living example of his leadership exhortations. Similarly, Templeton, Semler, and Carter palpably demonstrated integrity in their lives. Arguably this formed the basis for the greatest and most admirable parts of their leadership legacies.

Do you empower others to own their personal responsibility? Do you promote responsible self-leadership?

We pointed out earlier that integrity cannot exist if people do not own their personal responsibility, if they do not feel responsible for their actions. This is very much like saying that integrity cannot exist in a vacuum. When people are simply directed, by a controlling leader, on how to act in a situation involving moral issues, a moral vacuum is created. When people take action in the spirit of "following orders," it is just too easy to pass the buck to the external leader.

However, when those who implement a plan or strategy feel ownership of their actions, the potential for acting with conscience is established. Integrity is largely rooted in responsible action that requires people to feel responsible. The far-sighted leader will recognize that it is just as important, and often more important, to lead others so that a foundation for responsible action is laid, rather than focusing only on the technical quality of a decision. This leads us to another important question that gets to the heart of whether we can sincerely empower others.

Do you have the patience to let people learn, even through failure, when they are empowered?
When you first try more fully to involve and empower others, patience becomes very important. It is only natural that, at first, people will have a difficult time with the new challenges of being empowered. They will often make mistakes, and they will certainly do things differently than you would. Moses struggled in the face of the many poor choices his people made after they were freed from Egypt.

The key is to focus on learning and the long-term benefits that both you and your followers will enjoy. Our experience is that, when work operations are shifted from traditional forms of management to empowerment (such as self-managing team systems), performance tends to go down at first and may not completely recover for a year or two. This can be a difficult pill for a leader to swallow. But remember that the more you provide the learning opportunities and resources for people to succeed the sooner they will become more effective. In many cases, when leaders and organizations approach changes toward empowerment with patience and commitment, even in the face of temporary setbacks and mistakes, the results have been remarkable.

Justice

Finally, having considered leadership and integrity, we will shift the focus to the topic of justice. Here again are several questions to help you reflect on the role of justice in your life and leadership.

Are you willing to look beyond your own needs and stand up for others?

A primary lesson that flows from ancient wisdom, including that modeled by Moses, suggests that leadership, at its best, is practiced with a spirit of service. Perhaps this is the primary leadership legacy that former president Jimmy Carter has been demonstrating in his life. Few will argue that he was among the best American presidents, but he may well be the most admirable former president. His life has become a living model of service that challenges us all to look to the needs of others and to find our own way of serving.

Similarly, Sir John Templeton's primary motivation was to serve his clients. In fact, the reason he entered into financial investing, as opposed to pursuing his original calling of becoming a missionary, was that he felt he could provide greater service, given his talents for financial management. A handy guide for any leader to continually revisit is the question "How can I, and how will I, serve others?"

Do you involve others in the justice process? Do you open yourself for inspection, to be judged by those you lead?
Justice should be an open process that allows for checks and balances. At Semco, employees evaluate their bosses and their company.

Is your justice based on service rather than rules, procedures, and adversarial relations?
This question raises issues about the focus of your justice. It suggests that you consider what you hope to accomplish through the process of working toward justice. It suggests important additional questions. Do you seek justice as a way of serving others without primarily focusing on your own agenda and your own personal wants? Do you have an abundance mentality that rejoices with others' good fortune when it is deserved, even if you don't also directly benefit?

Do you put people first and "fighting for justice" second?
It is easy to get sucked into a just cause that threatens us directly. When we are put at risk by forces that do not recognize our legitimate rights, most of us will be moved to action to right the injustice. For many of us, seeing others treated unjustly strikes an emotional cord within us. The important challenge, sometimes overlooked, is that people need to be placed first, ahead of "the cause." Perhaps this frequent oversight is why our court systems are so overloaded with what many believe are trivial lawsuits.

Of course, some people take legal actions simply out of a sense of greed, a belief that they have a legal angle that makes financial gains likely. But many legal cases arise because people believe an injustice has occurred that must be righted. "It's the principle of the thing" is the common battle cry. In the end, however, justice becomes a legalistic contest in which winning is accorded more value than the people involved. Sometimes fighting is not the best answer; rather, collaborating with others (even our adversaries) to reach an innovative solution is more beneficial to all involved.

A good way to end our discussion is to ask perhaps the most important question of all. We believe that this is an essential question for any leader to ask who values integrity and is interested in promoting justice.

Is your leadership, and the justice it promotes, based more on giving or taking?

The Wisdom of Solomon

THE STORY OF SOLOMON

(Adapted from I Kings:1–11)

∾

Solomon was the son of David and the third king of Israel. From early in his life, he was noted for his songwriting talents and his expertise in natural history. He composed more than 1000 songs and 3000 proverbs (many in the Book of Proverbs of the Old Testament are attributed to him).

Solomon was a youth when his father, King David, died. Solomon found himself unprepared to be king. Solomon loved the Lord and the Lord found great favor in Solomon. "The Lord appeared to Solomon in a dream by night; and God said, 'Ask what I should give you.'" . . . and Solomon said, "'O Lord my God, you have made your servant king in place of my father David; although I am only a little child. . . . Give your servant . . . an understanding mind to govern your people, able to discern between good and evil; for who can govern this, your great people?'" (I Kings 3:5-9)

The Lord was greatly pleased and answered, "Because you have asked this, and have not asked for yourself long life or riches, or for the life of your enemies, but have asked for yourself understanding to discern what is right, I now do according to your word. Indeed I give you a wise and discerning mind; no one like you has been before you and no one like you shall arise after you. I give you also what you have not asked, both riches and honor all your life; no other king shall compare with you." (I Kings 3: 11-13)

Solomon's wisdom surpassed the wisdom of all the people of the east, and all the wisdom of Egypt. . . . People came from all the nations to hear the wisdom of Solomon; they came from all the kings of the earth who had heard of his wisdom. (I Kings 4:30, 34).

The most famous story of Solomon's wisdom is the story of a baby and the two women who claimed to be his mother.

Two women who were prostitutes came to the king and stood before him. The one woman said, ". . . this woman's son died . . . she got up in the middle of the night and took my son . . . and laid her dead son at my breast." . . . But the other woman said, "No, the dead son is yours, and the living son is mine."

. . . So the king said, "Bring me a sword . . . divide the living boy in two." But the woman whose son was alive said. . . "Please, my lord, give her the living boy; certainly do not kill him!" The other said, "It shall be neither mine nor yours; divide it." Then the king responded: "Give the first woman the living boy . . . she is his mother." All Israel heard of the judgment. . . and they stood in awe of the king, because they perceived that the wisdom of God was in him. (I Kings 3: 16-28)

Solomon's reign was very prosperous. The nation of Israel was at peace. The economy boomed, and literature and culture flourished. Because King David was never able to build a house for God during his reign of warfare, Solomon took advantage of the peace and built a house for the name of the Lord our God. It was a great temple, the finest building in the world at that time.

Two hundred thousand men labored for seven years to construct this monument. It was made of the finest wood, stone, carvings, and gold. In addition, Solomon built other great buildings, including his own magnificent palace. He built a huge fleet of ships to transport the gold, silver, ivory, and other precious items from afar. He built chariot cities that stabled 12,000 horses, included huge storage buildings, and provided houses for many of his wives.

Despite these successes of Solomon as King, his life later took a remarkable downturn. King Solomon loved women; in fact, he had 700 wives and 300 concubines. He was warned by God not to take a wife from a foreign culture, where the woman worshiped another god. These marriages would violate God's law (Deuteronomy 7:3-4). The beliefs of those wives would lead Solomon away from God. Solomon's heart was not true to God as he built a high place of worship for all his foreign wives "who offered incense and sacrificed to their gods." (I Kings 11: 7-8)

> Then the Lord was angry with Solomon, because his heart had turned away from the Lord, the God of Israel . . . (and) the Lord said to Solomon, "Since this has been your mind and you have not kept my covenant and my statutes that I have commanded you, I will surely tear the kingdom from you and give it to your servant. Yet for the sake of your father David I will not do it in your lifetime; I will tear it out of the hand of your son." (I Kings 11:9-12)

The Lord raised adversaries against Solomon during the final years of his forty-year reign over Israel. When Solomon died, he was buried in the City of David, and his son Rehoboam succeeded him.

WHEN WE SEE AND HEAR IN A DIFFERENT WAY

∞

Wisdom is a potent yet elusive concept. By now it is clear that seeking wisdom involves an often difficult, challenging, sometimes exciting, and transforming journey. This journey is loaded with paradox.

Wisdom contains both a profound intuitive dimension and a competent sense of the world. We have especially focused on an integrative and transcendent view of wisdom. We have suggested that this kind of wisdom can enable us to act in more effective ways. That is, as we act out of a deeper understanding, we are more effective.

Solomon serves as a powerful symbol for our quest. It is through his story, and through those of our other biblical characters, that we can connect the spiritual virtues to the wisdom of Solomon perspective, which we can incorporate into our daily work and lives.

We Possess the Seeds of Wisdom.

Solomon was thrust into the responsibility of kingship at an early age by the death of his father, King David. In the face of this loss and the struggles he now faced as a young king, one of the first things he did was ask God for wisdom in a dream. He prefaced his prayer for wisdom as follows: "And now, O Lord my God, you have made your servant (Solomon) king in place of my father David, although I am only a child; I do not know how to go out or come in. And your servant is in the midst of. . . a great people, so numerous they cannot be counted." (I Kings 3: 7-8). Solomon's own encounter with wisdom grew from the difficult catalyst of his father's death, and the faithfulness brought into and out of this event.

Wisdom was given to Solomon because he was faithful, and wise enough to ask for it. This suggests that Solomon was able to become wise because he possessed some degree of wisdom at the outset. We believe that this seeming paradox is true for each of us as well. To understand how to seek wisdom requires that we already possess it to some degree. Indeed, without some amount of wisdom, we lack the insight necessary to know what it is, let alone how to nurture it. Fortunately, each of us already possesses the seeds of wisdom and thus the potential to cultivate it in ourselves.

We grow in wisdom by being mindful of our focus in life and how that informs what we do. For Solomon, his focus was on God; he was faithful. He grew in prosperity as he remained faithful. However, Solomon was human and he too, like our other struggling, faithful, biblical characters, turned his focus away from God. He lost this focus when he accepted the other gods of his foreign wives. As a result, God raised up adversaries of Solomon during the last years of Solomon's life, and they overtook and divided his kingdom after Solomon's death (I Kings 11:1-12).

We cultivate wisdom as our faithful focus is strengthened through our own sensitivities of reason, reflection, and intuitive knowing.
Job introduces the importance of faith (faithfulness) and belief. The story of Job tells of a seemingly faithful man who tries consistently to do all the right things but still loses everything—his family, his wealth, and his health. Job is forced to delve deeply into his personal faith and his beliefs

about life, especially about God. Refined in the fires of personal tragedy and suffering, Job eventually forms a deeper and richer foundation of faith from which to live. Ultimately, Job regains his previous level of blessings and richness in his life, and becomes a more faithful, and presumably wiser, man.

We would prefer that the trials and difficulties be bypassed; if only there were some easier, less painful way to experience fully the power and necessity of faith, but it appears there is little substitute. Through the test of hardship, difficulty, and even tragedy, we may well obtain the wisdom we need if we will just stay present and engaged, even when we would most like to flee. The deeper sense of understanding we can gain from these life situations nourishes our seeds of wisdom.

We cultivate wisdom as our faithful focus is strengthened by facing life experiences with courage.

Wisdom, we have discovered, often emerges from living fully, especially during the struggles that force us out of our mindless routines. Struggle can provide the "stuff" that forces us to create and construct new forms of living.

To stay present to life's most difficult challenges, to work with them and learn from them, requires courage. David shows us the most obvious form of raw courage when, as a young boy, he faces a giant warrior with only a slingshot. He later displays a more subtle and deeper form of courage when he has to face his personal weakness and failure as a leader who abused power by coveting the beautiful Bathsheba.

Ironically, it seems clear that wisdom can be obtained only through fully engaging with life. We must keep our minds open and embrace our total life experience, even when it wounds us and sends us spinning into the agony and despair of loss, failure, and catastrophe. The parts of life from which we would most like to escape or avoid—the most difficult of our experiences, when we find ourselves deep in the pit of imperfect reality—can be the greatest sources of wisdom development. The biblical stories we have drawn from throughout this book emphasize this.

All the characters struggled, and all eventually gained in wisdom suited to their lives and their individual circumstances. Job had to struggle with tragic experiences that attacked the very core of what he believed was right and true. David struggled with his own lack of self-control in the face of lust for sexual passion and power. Ruth faced a hard moral choice that promised to separate her permanently from her own people, locking her into a foreign land with little hope of rising out of destitution. Moses faced the burden of leading a people who continually fell prey to temptations and weakness, while he himself felt unfit to lead. And Solomon was thrust into a kingship when little more than a child who felt hopelessly inadequate to meet the challenge. All of them ultimately endured as they drew on their deepest spiritual and personal resources.

We grow in wisdom as we face the challenges, ambiguity, and the unknowns of life, as did each of the biblical characters. We can learn from our own life experiences, especially those involving difficulty and struggle. It is through difficulty and struggle that spiritual nourishment is drawn to our seeds of wisdom. Without such challenge, our sense of self and wisdom would likely atrophy, as the physical body does without exercise. Thus, when we have a difficult time making sense of the world and our lives, especially in the face of what seem to be unnecessary hardships, we would do well to remember that our wisdom sources show us that struggle and crisis create fertile ground for growth in wisdom.

We cultivate wisdom as our faithful focus is strengthened by our desire to be in right relationships.

Encountering life in a way that enables us to grow in our faith and courage sets the stage for communal service and leadership. Throughout our life journey we can grow in wisdom as our faithful focus is strengthened by the understanding we gain from our faith traditions, the enduring essence of the scriptures, teachings, and rituals that have stood the test of time. It is our faith traditions that often call for us to be in community, to relate to one another, as we seek to realize a spiritual basis for our lives.

A compassionate stance involves looking beyond ourselves. Acting out of faith, and with courage, in the pursuit of wisdom enables the development of relationships and organizations that embrace or at least acknowledge the value of compassion. Ruth demonstrated a caring empathy for the predicament of Naomi, the older widow. She put her own welfare on the line to help Naomi. Acting with compassion requires a deep empathy for the struggles and suffering of others, which usually requires that we have struggled as well.

When we are able to focus on serving and supporting others, acts of compassion are made possible. When life keeps showering us with challenge, it is a solid foundation of personal faith and courage that enables us to rise beyond our own self-preservation and self-interest to act for the good beyond ourselves.

Ultimately, we arrive at a place where we can feel real compassion for others, where the welfare of our fellow human beings becomes an important priority. Indeed, compassion is arguably the virtue most important to wisdom. Nearly all the major religions and faith traditions of the world teach us to treat and care for others as we would like to be treated. Ruth embodies this lesson for us most poignantly.

We cultivate wisdom as our faithful focus is strengthened by our heightened sense of integrity and justice.

When people act out of faith, courage, and compassion, both individually and collectively, the potential for integrity and justice is enhanced. Moses continually found himself in difficult situations when the people of Israel displayed unfaithful behavior, but he never lost his faithful focus and his courageous and compassionate commitment to them. He stood up to the powerful Pharaoh of Egypt, demanding that the Israelites be set free. He stood up to his own people on many occasions when they chose destructive behaviors. Moses even found himself standing up to God when God was ready to destroy the Hebrew people.

It takes a faithful focus, along with courage and compassion, to look beyond our own immediate risks and welfare and to make hard choices that serve the wider good. It takes courage to lead with integrity and justice. And together, faith, courage, compassion, integrity, and justice will move us forward in our wisdom journey.

WHEN WE UNDERSTAND THAT WE ARE BUILDERS OF PROSPERITY

∞

Many times we have addressed the implications of individuals embracing a kind of spiritual wisdom for the "good of the people." All of our biblical characters acted on behalf of others with the intent of helping, supporting, building up, or leading. Cultivating wisdom is not an isolated process; wisdom calls us to be mindful of and responsible to "the people."

Wisdom becomes incorporated as we seek to develop the spiritual virtues in ourselves and to enact them through our interaction with others and through our leadership. That is, wisdom is fully realized as we encounter each other and build together for the good of all. We may be building new understanding between each other, new ideas for constructing better work, home, and community environments, or new ways of doing business, learning, and participating as global citizens.

Solomon, world-renowned for his wisdom, expressed his kingship largely through the construction of magnificent buildings. The buildings he created became monumental symbols of prosperous living, and they were driven by a wisdom-based perspective. It was the fruits of Solomon's wisdom—his creativity and prosperity—that captured the attention of his contemporaries and became legendary.

When Solomon asked God for wisdom, not personal riches and a long life, God responded that he would grant him wisdom. He added "I give you also what you have not asked, both riches and honor all your life; no other king shall compare with you" (I Kings 3:13). Thus, the great buildings of Solomon's reign serve as a monument to traditional ideas about prosperity and material wealth. However, if we reflect more deeply, we may face the question "for whom do you build up and why?"

Much of the challenge of building with a wisdom orientation is connected to the reconciliation of seemingly contradictory forces. Aaron Feuerstein, like Solomon, is a builder of prosperity. Feuerstein, however, found a way to build a strong business and offer a thriving work environment that extended beyond the bottom line.

In the Introduction, we presented the story of Aaron Feuerstein and his heroic behavior in the aftermath of a disastrous fire. Armed with his strong faith and the courage to challenge conventional wisdom, Feuerstein and his loyal employees helped Malden Mills rise from the ashes in a manner similar to the ancient spiritual tales that have inspired this book.

The story of a faithful man who wanted to "do the right thing" offers us a striking example of the relevance of ancient wisdom to modern management problems. We have explored several spiritual virtues that we believe contribute to wisdom, and have come full circle. It is fitting that we conclude as we began by returning to the business world of Aaron Feuerstein and the story of how he succeeded in what so many of us would like to do, to live and work from a solid base of spiritual virtues and to benefit ourselves and others in the process.[37]

It was a hot July morning as we arrived for our interview with Aaron Feuerstein at the headquarters of Malden Mills in Lawrence, Massachusetts. Our request to meet with Mr. Feuerstein was warmly received and, as we arrived at the site of the rebuilt mill, we began to understand the magnitude of his unselfish actions. Surrounding his gleaming state-of-the-art factory was a neighborhood comprised of empty storefronts, aging buildings, and other signs of economic hardship. It was not hard to imagine what the loss of 3000 jobs at Malden Mills would have done to this community, struggling to keep its head above water. From the moment we entered the company parking lot, we met Malden Mills employees who knew they were a part of something special. Their eyes reflected pride as they told us their role in the Malden Mills "miracle" and how they viewed Aaron Feuerstein as a beloved family member.

We were invited into Feuerstein's office, where he generously dismissed our concerns about time and invited his wife and coworker, Louise, to join our discussion. Feuerstein was extremely frank with us, and he quickly zeroed in on the relationship of spirituality and profitability. He told us ". . . to maximize the profitability. . . is essential in order to accomplish what I would like to accomplish. I would like, in my business, not only to win money, but also to win with my ideals, which are part of my faith. The treatment and sensitivity to our workers is critically important to me, and the welfare of the community is critically important to me.

"At the same time," he stated, "We are not a non-profit organization. The welfare, the growth, and the importance of the business are critically important to me." Feuerstein acknowledges that he has much yet to learn. "I must admit that, in my life, I've been taught many times that the adherence to that ideal of oneness alone, and not proper adherence to the reality of the business world, got me in trouble and pushed me backwards, so that what I had accomplished, I began to lose. So, I have to spend a great deal of time on what to do to win the business battle. Every time I forget to do that it brings terrible, terrible consequences."

Looking ahead, Feuerstein is very positive about Malden Mills' direction. "We have a vision here that we can have a first-class business that does first-class good on earth right here in Massachusetts." He recognizes that he will have to accomplish these lofty aims "knowing that we are paying many times more to our operators than you find elsewhere."

In order for Feuerstein to accomplish his ideal of combining solid business practice with doing good, there has to be a strong business plan at the business' foundation. Feuerstein has faith in his plan. "The business plan we have I believe is correct. . . . The plan will, in fact, in time, make us one of the very few who can succeed in the textile fabric business.

"We are not in the commodity product business depending on the cost of labor. We try to be in the business which differentiates us from commodity operators who can make goods cheaper than we do (in the Southern United States, in China, or in Mexico). How do I compete against them? I try to innovate to the best of my ability, much more so than they do, to make the quality and performance the best that man can think of. And, through innovation, we distance ourselves from those people who are operating with cheap labor.

"The other thing we do is that we take that innovation and build a recognizable brand, which is Polartec. We're making a fabric and we have what is called a component brand. We're not making the final product but we're making the goods that go into your suit. We're coming to Giorgio Armani and we're saying we have a brand that's a component of the item you're making. And we will make that so good and so innovative that it will allow you to have the kind of profitability to succeed in business. There's only one other guy who did it and that's Gore (Gore-Tex)." Feuerstein cited the Gore-Tex product as an example of a high-quality label that is marketed alongside the manufacturer's brand.

In reflecting on the critical role of his workers, Feuerstein says "I recognize that in any plan I've got to have that quality, and the worker, who becomes the most important asset I've got."

Feuerstein's wife, Louise, who played an important role herself in the rebuilding of Malden Mills, interjected and spoke briefly about additions to the new factory for the benefit of the workers. For example, after research, Louise Feuerstein recognized that "people who have natural light perform better." As the building was redesigned, the architect was asked to open all the windows. The huge windows had been boarded up because of the tremendous cost of replacement. They were upgraded with an expensive translucent glass that eliminated glare but let light through.

For three generations, the Feuerstein family had viewed their employees as their most valued asset. Because of this, the decision to rebuild despite the costs, the risks, and the traditional business values, was clear.

Louise Feuerstein went on to comment on her husband's core values. "I think it's a deep-seated Jewish belief that man is created in the image of God and that gives him a very positive view of life. So. . . instead of being negative and defeated, it's not in his genes to take that approach." She continued, "What I'd like to point out, however, is that Aaron's company did not just act this way with the onset of the fire. The fire made it public to the rest of the world, but in fact it had continued for almost 100 years through his family's business leadership."

Mrs. Feuerstein continued, "The employees knew his decision to rebuild was real. From that moment on, everyone stood behind it and became very energized." Aaron Feuerstein is philosophical about his celebrity status. "I became the celebrity because what I did automatically. . . isn't what the average American does today (but they would like to be able to do). I wouldn't have received the celebrity status unless the average American thought it was commendable."

Four years after the fire, Louise Feuerstein marveled, "We know how powerful rebuilding the mill was because every time we go to the airport or some public place, people come over and talk to us about it. So it touched a lot of people."

Acting with the faith of Job, the courage of David, the compassion of Ruth, and the integrity and justice of Moses, Aaron Feuerstein struggled along with his company and was able to rebuild for the good of his people.

We said our goodbyes and drove out of the parking lot. We were in quiet awe and appreciation for this man and his idea of oneness. And, we knew we had just caught a glimpse of ancient and contemporary wisdom in practice; we were witness to Wisdom Inc.*

∞

The ancient legacies of Job, David, Ruth, Moses, and Solomon are available to help light a fulfilling path for us as we face life's challenges. And, we also can draw insights of wisdom from the workplace stories shared here as well as those we encounter each day. However, ultimately we find ourselves standing where we began, confronting the relevance of wisdom for our lives.

Can we gain the wisdom we need to transform our lives? Can we face the challenge of putting wisdom into practice? Will our wisdom make a difference in the world?

---

*At the fifth anniversary of the fire, the Malden Mills "miracle" is still flourishing. While the number of employees has shrunk from the pre-fire high of 2800 to 1400 (due to the closing of its unprofitable upholstery division), the Polartec product has maintained its market leadership. Malden Mills continues to develop new, cutting-edge applications for a competitive advantage. Employee lawsuits from fire-related personal injury have been settled and Malden Mills currently operates small factories in Europe and sales offices in several major U.S. cities. Aaron Feuerstein continues his wise leadership of the company. For more information see *The Sunday Eagle Tribune,* December 10, 2000, pp A1, A8, A9 or www.eagletribune.com/news/stories/20001210/.

CAN WE LIVE, WORK,
AND LEAD WITH
THE WISDOM OF SOLOMON?

The act of searching is a core aspect of our history. Our search in business has led us to discoveries as varied as assembly lines, suggestion systems, highly empowered worker teams, and telecommuting. For example, the emergence of Japanese high-quality products in the 1980s made "Searching for Excellence" a rallying cry for a generation of leaders. The relentless pursuit of quality has lifted the United States from manufacturing mediocrity to technical superiority once more.

So, for what are we now searching? As the current wave of the Baby Boomer generation passes age fifty, many of the cultural anchors their parents and grandparents relied on for guidance and stability are in a state of flux. Company loyalty has all but disappeared, along with a sense of permanence in jobs and careers. The evening meal for many has yielded to single-serving, microwaved dinners. Children straggle in from school and countless other activities at all hours, while their often single or remarried, dual-career parents struggle to fulfill the limitless expectations of their jobs.

Yet it is precisely during these periods of cultural transition that we need to be most clear about what is truly meaningful in our lives. Since stability is not readily available from the external sources that have traditionally provided it, we need to be able to find our own lasting values and carry them along with us. Inspired by religious, spiritual, or ethical practices, these sets of values offer a kind of road map for our lives that transcends cultural change in work, family, church, and nation.

We may think of this highly personal set of operating principles as a life-support system that offers a capacity for "portable stability." What seems like an oxymoron at first, in truth becomes a kind of deeper, life-sustaining "spiritual backpack" that is carried intentionally and lovingly through the challenging terrain where we live and work.

In the real world we must be agile, and we have to pack lightly. Filling our spiritual backpacks with assets unnecessary for portable stability would only weight us down. If this were air travel, the spiritual backpack would be the carry-on item, the luggage we cannot afford to lose. The overhead compartment is as far as we allow ourselves to be removed from our pack.

What goes into our spiritual backpack? For many of us, a combination of stories, legends, and ethical principles from our religious/spiritual heritage are starting points for the search for meaning that continues our entire lives. Ironically, our greater exposure to the bountiful ideas of an increasingly multi-ethnic, multi-cultural society reveals perspectives that we would have missed out on a generation ago. Wisdom is out there, often in places where we least expect to find it. Frequently we return from a visit to a "foreign country" with a depth of understanding that we could not synthesize at our place of worship or in our library.

Spiritual issues *are* central to the challenges of worklife.

While business has increased standards of living and freed many to shift concerns from basic needs to higher issues, at the same time our vast cultural and technological change has moved us to seek sources of social stability, meaning, and purpose. When this coincides with our soul-searching personal struggle, the spiritual backpack becomes all the more important.

Efficiency and productivity can result from effective organizational structures and careful data analysis. But spirit and meaning can often spell the difference between an organization that thrives and one that merely exists. And yet, bringing our spirit to work seems to be contradictory to workplace values, which stress rational over spiritual behavior. "Leave the backpack at the door," we are told, and, when we do so, the untapped spiritual energy that can form the core of our leadership, mentorship, citizenship, and fellowship is muted.

In this book, we have honored the wisdom of Solomon and his Old Testament (Hebrew Bible) partners. We have begun filling the backpack with questions of faith, courage, compassion, integrity, justice, and, ultimately, wisdom. As you ask these questions in your own way, nurtured by the fertile fields of your own cultural, ethical, and religious background, we hope that the journeys taken by our fallible heroes from antiquity will offer you a vantage point for your own search for wisdom. We especially hope that this search will help equip you for exploring your personal struggles in ways that help you live a life that makes a difference to your work, to your family, and to this earth.

When the Queen of Sheba heard of the fame of Solomon . . . she came to test him with hard questions. . . . Solomon answered all her questions; there was nothing hidden from the king that he could not explain to her. When the Queen of Sheba had observed all the wisdom of Solomon, the house he had built, . . . there was no more spirit in her. So she said to the king, 'The report was true . . . of your accomplishments and of your wisdom . . . not even half had been told to me; your wisdom and prosperity far surpass the report I had heard." (I Kings 10: 1-7)

Thus King Solomon excelled all the kings of the earth in riches and in wisdom. The whole earth sought the presence of Solomon to hear his wisdom which God had put into his mind. (I Kings 10: 23-24)

NOTES

∞

1. Adapted from a story in Charles C. Manz, *The Art of Self-Leadership:Strategies for Personal Effectiveness in Your Life and Work* (Englewood Cliffs, NJ: Prentice-Hall, 1983, p. 53).

2. Personal interview between Aaron Feuerstein and his wife, Louise, and the authors, Robert Marx and Karen Manz, at Malden Mills, Lawrence, Massachusetts, July 16, 1999.

3. This case is drawn from several public speeches or interviews with Aaron Feuerstein. These include a speech Feuerstein delivered to over 5000 students at the University of Massachusetts Amherst, November 1996; A keynote speech Feuerstein presented at the First International Symposium on Spirituality in Business, March 1997, Boston; A documentary of Feuerstein and the Malden Mills fire, "Faith Under Fire," on *Chronicle*, WCVB-TV 5, 1996; and the article "Taking Good Care of Workers Pays Off," *The Arizona Republic*, January 23, 1997, pp. E1, E8.

4. "What Flames Could Not Destroy," Boston *Sunday Globe*, September 8, 1996.

5. *Chronicle* documentary.

6. UMass Amherst speech.

7. UMass Amherst speech.

8. "More Than a Factory," Boston *Globe*, December 8, 1996, p. 26.

9. Ibid.

10. *Chronicle* documentary.

11. "A Promise Kept: Mill Reopens," *The New York Times*, September 16, 1997.

12. The five biblical characters' stories are paraphrased by the authors, with references drawn from *HarperCollins Bible Dictionary* (HarperCollins, New York, 1996); *The Modern Reader's Dictionary of the Bible* (Association Press, New York, 1996); and *A Dictionary of the*

Bible (Oxford University Press, New York, 1996). The direct quotes of scripture are from the *New Revised Standard Version,* or the *New Living Translation,* Tyndale Press, as indicated by NLT.

13. "The Frugality Mentality," Boston *Sunday Globe,* June 25, 2000, p.A1.

14. "When You're Alone" by Bruce Springsteen, Copyright ©1987 by Bruce Springsteen (ASCAP).

15. Robinson, A.G. and Stern, S., *Corporate Creativity* (Berrett-Kohler, San Francisco, 1998).

16. Based on an interview with Dr. Barry Marshall, *20/20,* ABC News, August 4, 1995.

17. Ibid.

18. Ibid.

19. Donald D. Bowen, Roy J. Lewicki, T. Douglas Hall, and Francine S. Hall, *Instructor's Manual to Anonymity Experiences in Management and Organizational Behavior* (New York: John Wiley and Sons, Second Edition, 1982).

20. Ibid., pp. 168-175.

21. From the *Rabbinical Assembly Manual,* p. 134.

22. Story circulated on the Internet; unable to track down an original source.

23. "In Pursuit of Affluence at a High Price, " *The New York Times,* February 2, 1999.

24. This story was relayed to Karen Manz by retired Ford executive Lewis Padgett, Jr., Oct. 10, 1998, Farmington, Michigan.

25. For more information on the story of Dave Thomas of Wendy's, see the article "Dave's Way" by Carrie Shook, *Forbes,* March 9, 1998, pp. 126-27.

26. Jon Bowen, "True Confessions," *Runners' World,* March 1999, p. 128.

27. "What Dreams May Come," *Interscope Communications,* 1998.

28. Ann Landers, "Nurses in Hospitals Say the Profession Is Hurting," Detroit *Free Press,* October 11, 1998, p. 2G. Permission granted by Ann Landers and Creators Syndicate.

29. Leonard L. Berry, *Discovering the Soul of Service: The Nine Drives of Sustainable Business Success* (New York, The Free Press, 1999, p. 243).

30. For more information on Jimmy Carter as a presidential leader and as an active ex-president working in humanitarian causes, see Henry P. Sims, Jr. and Charles C. Manz, *Company of Heroes* (New York, Wiley, 1996, pp. 5-7).

31. For more information on SuperLeadership and how to put it into practice, see Charles C. Manz and Henry P. Sims Jr., *SuperLeadership: Leading Others to Lead Themselves* by (New York, Berkley Books, 1990), and *Company of Heroes: Unleashing the Power of Self-Leadership* (New York, Wiley, 1996).

32. For more information on Ricardo Semler's leadership at Semco, see "Managing Without Managers," *Harvard Business Review*, Sept.–Oct., 1989, pp.76-84, and *Maverick* (New York, Warner, 1993) both written by Ricardo Semler.

33. Semler, "Managing Without Managers," p. 84.

34. Frank O'Donnell, "When Workers Are Bosses," *Washington Post*, Sept. 14, 1993, p. B–2.

35. *Servant leadership* is leadership by serving others rather than by directing or controlling. For further reading, see Robert K. Greenleaf, *On Becoming a Servant-Leader* (Jossey-Bass, San Francisco, 1997).

36. "The Principle of Maximum Pessimism," *Forbes*, January 16, 1995, pp.67–71,74.

37. Personal interview between Aaron Feuerstein and his wife, Louise, and the authors, Robert Marx and Karen Manz, at Malden Mills, Lawrence, Massachusetts, July 19, 1999.

INDEX

∞

ABOUT THE AUTHORS

Charles C. Manz, Ph.D., is a speaker, consultant, and best-selling business author. He is currently the Charles and Janet Nirenberg Professor of Business Leadership in the Isenberg School of Management at the University of Massachusetts Amherst. Dr. Manz's work has been featured on radio and television, as well as in the *Wall Street Journal, Fortune, U.S. News & World Report, Success,* and several other national publications. He received the prestigious Marvin Bower Fellowship at the Harvard Business School, which is "awarded for outstanding achievement in research and productivity, influence, and leadership in business scholarship."

He is the author of over 100 articles and 12 books, including the bestsellers *Business Without Bosses: How Self-Managing Teams Are Building High-Performing Companies, The Leadership Wisdom of Jesus: Practical Lessons For Today,* and the Stybel-Peabody prize winner, *SuperLeadership: Leading Others to Lead Themselves.*

Dr. Manz has served as a consultant for many organizations, including 3M, Ford, Motorola, Xerox, the Mayo Clinic, Procter & Gamble,GeneralMotors, American Express, Arthur Anderson, Banc One, the American Hospital Association, the American College of Physician Executives, and the U.S. and Canadian governments.

Karen P. Manz studies, writes, and speaks in the areas of spirituality and religion, adult learning, and social issues in contemporary culture. She was conference coordinator for the national conference "Going Public with Spirituality in Work and Higher Education" at the University of Massachusetts at Amherst, June, 2000 (www.umass.edu/spiritual_conf/). She has been an active learner and participant in the area of spirituality for many years and is currently participating in an ecumenical Academy for Spiritual Formation.

She holds a masters degree in higher education and she pursued doctoral studies in the social anthropology of religion, education and community at Arizona State University. In addition, she studied education at the Graduate School of Education at Harvard University, and religion at the School of Theology at Claremont.

Karen P. Manz has served as a researcher, writer, and instructor in the areas of adult learning and adult learning systems. She has co-authored articles in a variety of journals and periodicals and is co-author of the book *For Team Members Only: Making Your Workplace Team Productive and Hassle Free*. She has also served as a consultant to organizations in both the public and private sectors.

Robert D. Marx, Ph.D., is an Associate Professor of Management at the University of Massachusetts at Amherst. He is the co-author of *Management Live! The Video Book*. His research efforts have focused on the problem of skill retention following management development programs. He has published on the topic of relapse prevention in management training in numerous journals. He was co-editor of the *Journal of Management Development*'s special issue on the use of video in management education.

He was named the 1991 recipient of the Bradford Outstanding Educator Award from the Organizational Behavior Teaching Society. He is currently chairman of the board of the Organizational Behavior Teaching Society.

He has recently taught MBA classes in St. Petersburg, Russia, and at the Athens Laboratory for Business Administration in Greece, and was invited to be a lecturer at the Graduate School of Business Leadership, UNISA (University of South Africa, Pretoria). He consults with numerous organizations on issues of leadership, teamwork, communication, and improving skill retention in management training.

Christopher P. Neck, Ph.D., is currently an associate professor of management at Virginia Polytechnic Institute and State University. His research specialties include executive/employee health/fitness, self-leadership, leadership, group decision-making processes, and self-managing team performance. He has published over fifty journal articles and book chapters and three books, including *Mastering Self-Leadership: Empowering Yourselves For Personal Excellence* and *Medicine for the Mind: Healing Words to Help You Soar.*

Dr. Neck has been cited in numerous national publications including the *Washington Post, The Los Angeles Times, Entrepreneur Magazine, Runner's World,* and *New Woman* magazine. Additionally, as a faculty member at Virginia Tech, Dr. Neck teaches a management practice course to over 550 students. He has received numerous teaching awards at Virginia Tech including the 1996, 1998, and 2000 Outstanding Teacher of The Year Award.

Some of the organizations who have participated in Dr. Neck's management development training, self-leadership training, and/or keynote speeches include Busch Gardens, Clark Construction, the United States Army, Crestar, American Family Insurance, Sales and Marketing Executives International, America West Airlines, American Electric Power, W. L. Gore & Associates, Dillard's Department Stores, and Prudential Life Insurance.

Postscript

This author team represents Protestant, Catholic, and Jewish religious heritage. Our ages span the thirties, forties, and fifties. Among us, we have been active in religious life in all regions of the United States, from the East Coast to the Pacific Northwest, and the Desert Southwest to the Deep South. We have all struggled with "trying to do the right thing" in our work and lives.

Berrett-Koehler Publishers

BERRETT-KOEHLER is an independent publisher of books, periodicals, and other publications at the leading edge of new thinking and innovative practice on work, business, management, leadership, stewardship, career development, human resources, entrepreneurship, and global sustainability.

Since the company's founding in 1992, we have been committed to supporting the movement toward a more enlightened world of work by publishing books, periodicals, and other publications that help us to integrate our values with our work and work lives, and to create more humane and effective organizations.

We have chosen to focus on the areas of work, business, and organizations, because these are central elements in many people's lives today. Furthermore, the work world is going through tumultuous changes, from the decline of job security to the rise of new structures for organizing people and work. We believe that change is needed at all levels—individual, organizational, community, and global—and our publications address each of these levels.

We seek to create new lenses for understanding organizations, to legitimize topics that people care deeply about but that current business orthodoxy censors or considers secondary to bottom-line concerns, and to uncover new meaning, means, and ends for our work and work lives.

See next pages for other books from Berrett-Koehler Publishers

More books from Berrett-Koehler

Also by Charles Manz!

The Leadership Wisdom of Jesus

Practical Lessons for Today

Charles Manz

Remarkably contemporary and resonant with the approaches taken by today's most successful leaders. This book offers guidance that enables leaders and followers to maintain their integrity, live on a higher plane, and reach their goals.

Paperback, 188 pages • ISBN 1-57675-066-3 CIP
Item #50663-365 $14.00

What Would Buddha Do at Work?

101 Answers to Workplace Dilemmas

Franz Metcalf and BJ Gallagher Hateley

What Would Buddha Do at Work? presents 101 typical issues that people struggle with daily, ranging from coping with difficult bosses and serving customers to being creative and offering leadership. In response, the authors pass along Buddhist wisdom that will guide readers to "enlightened" answers that are both spiritual and practical.

Hardcover, 180 pages • ISBN 1-5697-5300-8 CIP
Item #53008-365 $16.95

A Higher Standard of Leadership

Lessons from the Life of Gandhi

Keshaevan Nair

Through illustrative examples from Gandhi's life and writings, Keshavan Nair identifies commitments—to conscience, openness, service, values, and reduced personal attachments—and describes the courage and determination necessary to work and lead by them.

Paperback, 174 pages • ISBN 1-57675-011-6 CIP
Item #50116-365 $16.95

Berrett-Koehler Publishers
PO Box 565, Williston, VT 05495-9900
Call toll-free! **800-929-2929** 7 am-12 midnight
Or fax your order to 802-864-7627
For fastest service order online: **www.bkconnection.com**

Also by Charles Manz!

The New SuperLeadership

Leading Others to Lead Themselves

Charles C. Manz and Henry P. Sims, Jr.

"SuperLeadership" teaches how to "lead others to lead themselves." Based on the bestselling *SuperLeadership,* this book emphasizes a how-to approach, providing practical guidance for implementing SuperLeadership and featuring contemporary examples from the high-tech and knowledge-based business sectors.

Hardcover, 280 pages • ISBN: 1-57675-105-8 CIP
Item #51058-365 $27.95

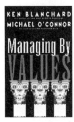

Managing By Values

Ken Blanchard and Michael O'Connor

Managing by Values provides a practical game plan for defining, clarifying, and communicating an organization's values and ensuring that its practices are in line with those values throughout the organization.

Hardcover, 140 pages • ISBN 1-57675-007-8 CIP
Item #50078-365 $20.00

Audiotape, 2 cassettes/3 hrs. • ISBN 1-57453-146-8
Item #31468-365 $17.95

Bringing Your Soul to Work

An Everyday Practice

Cheryl Peppers and Alan Briskin

This book addresses the gap between our inner lives and the work we do in the world. Case studies, personal stories, reflective questions, and concrete applications guide readers through the challenges inherent in the workplace.

Paperback, 260 pages • ISBN 1-57675-111-2 CIP
Item #51112-365 $16.95

Berrett-Koehler Publishers
PO Box 565, Williston, VT 05495-9900
Call toll-free! **800-929-2929** 7 am-12 midnight

Or fax your order to 802-864-7627
For fastest service order online: **www.bkconnection.com**

Spread the word!

Berrett-Koehler books and audios are available at quantity discounts for orders of 10 or more copies.

The Wisdom of Solomon at Work
Ancient Virtues for Living and Leading Today

Charles C. Manz, Karen P. Manz, Robert D. Marx, and Christopher P. Neck

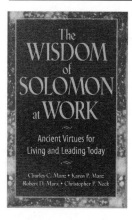

Hardcover, 150 pages
ISBN: 1-57675-085-X CIP
Item #5085X-365 $20.00

To find out about discounts on orders of 10 or more copies for individuals, corporations, institutions, and organizations, please call us toll-free at (800) 929-2929.

To find out about our discount programs for resellers, please contact our Special Sales department at
(415) 288-0260; Fax: (415) 362-2512. Or email us at bkpub@bkpub.com.

Berrett-Koehler Publishers
PO Box 565, Williston, VT 05495-9900
Call toll-free! **800-929-2929** 7 am-12 midnight

Or fax your order to 802-864-7627
For fastest service order online: **www.bkconnection.com**